W9-AVK-633

compelled to
WRITE
to you

Letters on Faith, Love, Service, and Life

compelled to

to you

christopher de vinck and
elizabeth m. mosbo verhage

UPPER
ROOM BOOKS®
NASHVILLE

Cover & interior design: Gore Studio, Inc.
Cover photo: © Photodisc, Inc.
First printing: 2001
The Upper Room® Web site: http://www.upperroom.org

Library of Congress Cataloging-in-Publication Data

de Vinck, Christopher, 1951–
    Compelled to Write to You: Letters on Faith, Love, Service, and Life /
by Christopher de Vinck, Elizabeth M.Mosbo VerHage
        p.   cm.
    ISBN 0-8358-0940-4
    1. de Vinck, Christopher, 1951—Correspondence.   2. VerHage,
Elizabeth M.Mosbo—Correspondence.   3. Spiritual Life I. VerHage,
Elizabeth. II. Title.
BX4705.D473 A4 2001
282'.092—dc21   00-043531

Printed in the United States of America

CHRIS
to Roe

LIZ
to the many who have helped me explore
"the upside-down kingdom," and to
those few who have made me, me:

Bo
My Parents

Peter

When we dare to speak from the depth of our heart to the friends God gives us, we will gradually find new freedom within us and new courage to live our own sorrows and joys to the full.

—Henri J. M. Nouwen
Can You Drink the Cup?

contents

introduction

As a writer I receive many letters each year from people who stumble upon my work and wish to say hello, or who wish to say that something I wrote made them nod their heads in agreement, or that something I said moved them in a particular way that compelled them to write to me.

I know writers who refuse unsolicited letters and return them unopened. Many writers return a form letter with a photocopied signature stating that they are too busy, too important, or too famous to take the time to respond personally to what comes to them in the mail. And then there are the writers who answer all their mail with attention.

Last week my wife and I spent a day at the New Jersey shore, Point Pleasant, an appropriate name for a place by the ocean. As we walked along the sand, accompanied by the waves churning at our feet, I noticed a small, low-flying plane making its way toward us along the coast. I said to Roe, "Watch this." As the plane approached, I threw up my right arm and gave the pilot a wide wave. Suddenly the distant plane's wings dipped back and forth. "Isn't that great?" I said. "He sees us!" And the plane continued on its way.

I like that: waving to a stranger from a distance and seeing the stranger wave back. We do this at parting ships, at passing trains. There are moments in our lives when we like to acknowledge the existence of another person, being connected to that person simply because we too are human beings on the earth, living similar lives of struggle and mild victories.

People on motorcycles wave to each other as they pass on the highway. Archaeologists marvel at the discovery of a sentence carved into stone. Astronauts leave a plaque on the moon for others to find someday.

As a literature teacher for twenty years, I wanted my students to understand the extended messages writers leave behind in their poems, novels, and plays. Scout stepped from the porch of Boo's house in *To Kill a Mockingbird* and spoke to us about fear and childhood and lost memories. In *The Great Gatsby,* Jay Gatsby reached across the bay as he tried to hold the light of love in the very palm of his hand. George, in John Steinbeck's *Of Mice and Men,* tried to protect Lenny. He tried to protect us all as he made excuses for his odd friend.

In my writing career, I have received letters from the president of the United States, cardinals, bishops, lawyers, teachers, farmers, poets, novelists, members of congress, television personalities, newspaper editors, mothers, welders, salespeople, veterans, brokers, doctors, carpenters, ambassadors, scholars, prisoners.

I answer all my letters. Sometimes I include an essay or a photograph or a bit of news about the family or a forecast of the night's weather. I try to make a connection.

In the letters I receive I find a unifying thread, a common purpose that connects them all: the desire people have to corroborate what is in their hearts with what they have found in my books. People tell me things about their failed marriage or about the birth of their grandson. They send me pictures of their children at birthday parties and poems they have written. I receive little prayer cards with dried flowers attached, CDs from musicians, videotapes from artists. People send me stones or leaves or even acorns from places they have loved. A man who owns an oil company sent my wife and me a wheel of cheese. I once received a bleeding heart plant because I wrote how I destroyed, by accident, the bleeding heart plant in my garden many years ago.

Here is a typical letter I receive in the mail:

Dear Chris:
Last week the girls and I went for an evening walk on the
country road where we live. We put Jessica in the stroller that
I guided while Shannon pushed it along the bumpy path.
When our eyes became adjusted to the darkness, Shannon
threw back her head and was mesmerized by the new path in
front of her...the night sky. There was a noticeable wind that
caused the clouds to cover and then release the moonlight as
we walked. Shannon held onto the stroller handle and had
the confidence to walk with her nose pointed up to the stars,
knowing that since I was directing her journey, she would be
safe. With her head thrown back she said, "What's up there
Mom?" Simple question—difficult to answer. We started
naming the things we saw—the clouds, the moon and stars
—and then she said there's lots of things we can't see that
are up there, too. Not many people know about things that
aren't visible. I was surprised when she began naming things
that she knew were there ... "God and the angels and John
Glenn." Yes, I thought, sandwiched in between the clouds
and the stars are God and John Glenn.

Before our walk we had listened to the news reports of
John Glenn's return to space. With Shannon's face fixed on
the stars, she said, "God and the angels are always watching
over us, so they must be there, too." We said good night to
Mr. Glenn before we stepped back in the house.

I write about little things, and I receive grand things in the
mail. *"What's up there, Mom?"*

I write stories about my son whispering in the dark as I
adjust his blankets: "I love you, Dad." I write about my
daughter wishing to be Mary in the Christmas pageant, but
she was picked only to be an angel: "I don't want to be an
angel, Daddy." I write about my wife, Roe, and how much I
like watching her comb her hair in the morning as she
reminds me to drive Michael to his fencing lessons. I write
about turtles in the yard of my father or about sitting on
top of silos with my student as he speaks about his future

and his doubts. I write about what is lost to me, the child I was, the people I once loved, the places I will never visit again. People seem to recognize something of themselves in what I write. I say this without boast, without pride. I say this with acceptance and confidence. A writer comes, eventually, to understand the type of writer he or she really is.

I wrote a small essay for *The Wall Street Journal* about my mentally disabled, blind brother named Oliver who lived for thirty-two years in his bed in the house where I grew up. That article propelled my writing career, though I did not realize it at the time. And hundreds of people wrote to me about that essay.

Such a surprise fringe benefit of being a writer: People write letters to you. People respond. People lift their hands and wave back and forth. The impulse to write is in us all. The impulse to react to what we recognize as our central selves is a powerful force that gives us a sense of belonging: a sense that we too are important and made for this earth, made to survive and to make a difference.

We swirl in and out of jobs, trains, television programs, worries, bills, anger, defeats, victories. We laugh in the afternoon with a son on the front steps and toss in our beds at night because we cannot sleep. The size of our own failures consumes us, and our shadows haunt us; yet…there are profound moments too. A surge of recognition that there is an inner power, something turning inside that makes us aware that we are powerful, beautiful, happy, significant, at ease with the world and with what the world tries to do to us when we are close to defeat.

I write because of the churning self that brings up notions of spring and hints of a merciful God—that self born to stick his hand into the mix of a given life and pull out a daughter's learning to swim, a raspberry from my father's garden, a wife sleeping next to me.

See? This is why people write me letters. They know such mixture. They too hold their babies in the darkness and sing to them. They too know the summer sounds of a

sister calling them into the lake. They too smell the bread
in the baker's shop, run their hands along the sleeves of a
favorite sweater. They wave to the pilot and hope he will tip
the wings of his airplane. "Hello! Hello, up there! Hello!"

In September of 1998, I received a letter from a college
student that began, "Dear Christopher de Vinck: I just finished reading your book *The Power of the Powerless* and was
compelled to go into my room and write to you. I felt that I
had to connect with you and respond to what you had written, not just read your words and absorb them silently."

We are not creatures of silence. We need to be heard.
We are compelled to express what it is that is innately *us*.
When I received the first letter from Liz Mosbo, I read it
again and again for I recognized in it what I have heard for
twenty years in one way or another from the many letters
I have received.

I realized from my growing correspondence with Liz
that she was asking universal questions that young people
ask. She was articulating what so many students are looking
for in their own lives: a way to move forward, a way to
make a difference, a way to be. In all my years teaching, I
have sensed that my students long for advice, guidance, and
support; they long to be encouraged. Where do young people go these days for such advice? Television? Movies?
Newspapers? Parents? Friends? Teachers? God?

How we come to our own understanding of who we are
is a single journey. We each have to make our own way. In
my correspondence with Liz, I realized that I was offering
her questions to consider. I was offering her a place where
she could experiment with different ideas about her future.
I was offering her friendship and guidance and love and
hope and corroboration that she was on a significant path.
And I realized that she was offering the same to me.

Once when I was a boy and it was summer, my best
friend Johnny and I were swimming in the local lake. Suddenly, black clouds gathered and the lifeguard issued a
warning. Johnny and I swam out from the water, grabbed

our towels, and ran to our bikes. We were heading home, trying to beat the thunderstorm. I will never forget riding down Crescent Avenue, peddling hard, laughing with Johnny up ahead of me as the distant thunder roared. Johnny looked back and waved, "Come on, Chrissy! Come on!" We beat the storm and drank Kool-Aid in his kitchen as the rain and thunder and lightning danced in defeat outside, where the trees bent under the wind.

I answered Liz Mosbo's first letter with vigor, realizing that I was waving back, sending through the mail the same invitation: "Come on, Liz! Before the rain gets us!"

Rainer Maria Rilke, in his famous little book, *Letters to a Young Poet*, wrote "Love your solitude and bear with sweet-sounding lamentation the suffering it causes you. For those who are near you are far, and that shows it is beginning to grow wide about you. And when what is near you is far, then your distance is already among the stars and very large; rejoice in your growth, in which you naturally can take no one with you."

With each letter I received from Liz Mosbo, and with each response, I realized more and more that this young woman was asking the right questions: What of faith? What of the future? What of vocation? What of marriage? I also realized that she was right there with Johnny and me as we tried to beat the storm. We all try to beat the storm, and when we find someone who will ride beside us, we tend to laugh or wave or send letters.

I hope these letters teach you to "love your solitude and bear with sweet-sounding lamentation the suffering it causes you." I hope these letters convince you to take risks in love. Extend your hand across the distance of your suffering, your loneliness, your doubts, and discover a merciful God. Liz Mosbo wrote me a letter because she felt something inside of her that she could not define, but she could recognize. Something I wrote by happenstance compelled her to write to me. This inner jolt that compels us to move forward is the secret joy we cannot name, the constant doubt we dare not confront. It is what we call grace or God or daughter or husband or poetry or silos. We create evidence of an inside self, a soul-self, but we cannot see it directly.

Letters are like artifacts, things we might keep in the cupboard behind the sugar as reminders of plain certitude we cannot define but recognize in the handwriting.

May these letters on your lap find their way to your cupboard, compel you to wave to the stranger in the distance, and help you share your soul-self with a friend. Good night, John Glenn.

Letter One

The Upside-Down Kingdom

I want to claim the upside-down kingdom as my sanctuary, my way in this world. But this world is passing on topsy-turvy values to my generation. We are inundated with selfishness and ambition, lust and short-term satisfaction. I need glimpses into the upside-down kingdom every now and then to remind myself that not everyone lives like that, not everyone is fooled; real power is not to be found on that scale.

Dear Christopher de Vinck:

I just finished reading your book *The Power of the Powerless*
and was compelled to go into my room and write to you.
I felt that I had to connect with you and respond to what
you had written, not just read your words and absorb
them silently.

This past August I began my senior year at North Park
University in Chicago. You may remember speaking here
last year at our morning chapel service. I was deeply moved
and excited about what you said. It is rare to hear someone
who is "a slice above the crowd" speak so radically about
sacrifice and powerlessness. I was encouraged and moti-
vated to know that people still really believe in that and
that compassion is not limited to fiction writing or to
quotes that we frame and hang on the walls. I have a copy
of the *The Wall Street Journal* article about Oliver glued in
my quote book.

Almost by accident I bought your book at a Christian
bookstore this summer. As I was walking to another section
of the store, your name caught my eye. The book was on
sale, so I had to buy it right then and there. God knew that
I needed that book, and I devoured the slim volume with
much thought and with pauses to try to make sure that I
was really digesting all that you were actually saying.

I don't have a gripping story involving a handicapped
loved one or a background rife with struggle to tell you
about. My story is simple and much more basic than the
things that you and many others in the book have dealt

with. But I am stuck in this phase that I am dealing with presently, and for some reason I feel like this is what I am supposed to write to you about. Ironically, sometimes the most basic struggles are the most important ones.

I am from a middle-class Christian family that ate supper together every night and still sometimes snuggles together in bed, even though my brother is sixteen and I am twenty-one years old. We watched musicals and ate grilled cheese sandwiches a lot growing up. My mom sang to us, showed us how to make Christmas spritz cookies, and always gave of herself. My dad is quiet and sensitive, and I am still taken aback when he doesn't know the answer to something that I ask him. He made us a sandbox out of a tractor tire that sat near the raspberry bushes. My parents never missed a piano recital, school play, volleyball game, or choir concert that I was in. I really can't remember a single one that they didn't come to. We used to play board games like *Perquackey*® and *Clue*® for hours and make homemade ice cream. I never, ever doubted that they loved me or that they would always love me. And I took them for granted, I think.

My family also struggles with a lot of things; I think that every family does. My town is a pretty safe, moral, sheltered town with decent, educated, professional people; most parents of my friends are well-educated and employed at our world-renowned hospital or thriving computer company. The social infrastructure of my town seemed to rest on being educated, organized, and socially adjusted. So I became educated, organized, and socially adjusted. I also knew that other endeavors like volunteer work, social issues, and church life were very important to me as well (though they were secondary and fit into the cracks of my schedule). In my mind I renamed the goals of "status and power" with labels like "being influential so that you can help more people," or "making a lot of money so that you can give it away to those who need it."

I think I always felt as if I were extraordinary: I was used to being the best at a lot of things. I thought I was more grounded and more genuine than most people because I thought so much about how power and fame and status don't make people happy. And yet I still desired it in some part of my mind. Those things still were attractive to me.

Here in college I have become more mature and realistic (though, in many ways, I am still a very unrealistic, idealistic person). I am not the best—at anything, really—anymore. I have quite a few friends, but I don't know everyone and not everyone knows me. I sing in the choir, but I don't have the solo parts. I am very involved at the service organization on campus, but I am not the director. I am a good student, but I will not graduate with top honors.

I think that these experiences have shown me that I am not extraordinary, at least not any more than each person on the planet is extraordinary. Because what is ordinary? What is average? Even people who seem shallow and boring and selfish often have a wealth to offer if they are encouraged with compassion and sincerity. Even those of us who seem outgoing and content and capable have a wealth of problems and questions that are not always solvable with education, organization, or social skills.

So what I am learning from your book and from God lately is that I am still a really selfish person. It is easier to love people in a theoretical sense while on a mission trip or in the spotlight or when you get fringe benefits and it makes you feel good. Love is, by definition, putting others before yourself. That means caring about what they care about—before, above, and beyond what I care about. Friendships teach you that; dating teaches you that; my parents and my brother teach me that.

So why do I still strain against the sacrificial aspects of love? Why do thoughts like these rush through my brain:

If I listen to this person I will never finish my paper, and she always complains about the same problems, anyway.

This is risky to disagree with the popular group's way of defining Christianity. Is it really worth it?

Why can't my parents give me as much money as other parents do?

Why am I not recognized for being kind and giving or for trying? Why isn't that noticed?

There are days when it really bothers me that I seem to be the only one doing something or that nobody seems to recognize what I am doing. These are clear signs that I still think that I am extraordinary and should receive certain things. I would rather be able to get joy just from giving, not making a mental check mark every time I give sacrificially; but that is hard. It is much harder than being organized, educated, and socially adjusted. I have to keep choosing to give every single day, over and over again. Jesus said, "Those who want to save their life will lose it, and those who lose their life for my sake will find it. For what will it profit them if they gain the whole world but forfeit their life?" (Matt. 16:25–26a).

It is hard for me to put into tangible terms what I feel. I read about it and write about it; I think about it and mull it over in discussions with my friends. Do I want to be without, to be overlooked, to be beneath and behind others? Do I want to disregard what I am "entitled" to and what I think my rights are? Do I want to be satisfied with being ordinary, because no one really is ordinary after all? How ordinary is your family? your mother? Oliver? How ordinary is my family? my mother? my brother? The extraordinary can only appear when you are unaware of it creeping up on you; maybe chasing it and shouting for it disturbs the peace by which "extraordinariness" is nurtured. Our consumer-oriented society doesn't understand this.

I went to Bible camp every summer—another thing that my parents gave to me. The theme for one summer was hung on crepe paper in the log chapel: "The upside-down kingdom." I have always remembered that phrase and somehow believe in the ideal that Jesus spoke of when he talked about losing your life to gain it. It scares me sometimes when the values of the business world or the scale of outward attractiveness comfort me. I want to claim the upside-down kingdom as my sanctuary, my way in this world. But this world is passing on topsy-turvy values to my generation. We are inundated with selfishness and ambition, lust and short-term satisfaction. I need glimpses into the upside-down kingdom every now and then to remind myself that not everyone lives like that, not everyone is fooled; real power is not to be found on that scale.

Thank you for a giving me a vision of what the upside-down kingdom looks like. I am so attracted to your viewpoint and to your ability to notice the small and yet truly powerful things—and then to write it out as well as you do. I am appreciating the power of words more and more as I read and write and search for the right words. I want to be a part of all that you have written about and believe in. I want to notice my own extraordinary family and my own selfishness, not in order to scold myself, but in order to grow and to let the peace of extraordinariness blossom. I hope that you understand all this. Somehow I think that you will. If you ever come to our college again, I would like to talk to you and thank you and just enjoy another who loves and serves and sees, really sees. Thank you. God bless you and your extraordinary family.

Liz Mosbo

Letter Two

The
Inside self

Liz, we all struggle with an inside self....
We feel something boiling inside of us, but no
one notices or understands. Sometimes we feel
silly for even feeling what we feel because we
do not want to act as if we are special and
different and amazing.

Dear Liz Maybo:

I have been meaning to write ever since your letter of September 19 arrived yesterday afternoon. Before I could find a free moment I did a book signing in Manhattan, picked up my son at Rutgers for the weekend, attended my younger son's soccer game, attended my daughter's marching band performance, cooked dinner, answered my e-mail, washed dishes, shopped for shirts, and retrieved the car at the repair shop. So, finally I can give the time your letter deserves. And by the way, I feel a bit hopeful that I can respond in a way that will make a significant difference to you, for your letter is, in many ways, a touchstone for me. It shows again that what I write about, what I believe does exist in the world, does indeed exist.

You see, Liz, for you to respond to what I write makes me realize that what I feel and see and dream of and hope for is real, because it is the dream of others too.

Try not to hold heroes up to a bright light, for what you see in those you admire is really you... your light. What you found in my book was yourself, not much of me. A book is a mirror. When we look at our physical selves we can say, yes, I recognize the physical features of my body; yes, that is who I am on the surface. But there is no mirror for the inside part of us, except other people and books. The people who love you are reflections of who you are. They see something wonderful in you and react. The books that you select that are meaningful out of all the books you read suggest who you are on the inside. Lucky the author when, every now and then, someone writes and says, "Hey, me too!" Your wonderful letter was a "me too" letter... you also feel and see and believe what I see and feel and believe.

23

I was pleased to see your response to my book *The Power of the Powerless*. It is not a book about disabilities. You found the very center of what I was writing. The book is about struggle and how we tend to that struggle. No, you may not have endured the pain that my mother did when she discovered Oliver's afflictions. No, you may not have experienced the heart-crushing stories that I recount in the book; but you are struggling, and you felt the struggle of people in what I wrote. Perhaps you even detected that I too struggle. We all do, Liz; we all struggle with an inside self. For some people that struggle is overt. It was obvious on one level to see what my mother's struggles were just by looking at Oliver; but what about people who live with inside struggles, turmoils of the heart? That struggle is not so obvious. And we live in a world where many people do not like to dig within themselves to identify this inner war or even to acknowledge its existence. There is something sad about that, and it makes people like us feel, well, alone even more. We feel something boiling inside of us, but no one notices or understands. Sometimes we feel silly for even feeling what we feel because we do not want to act as if we are special and different and amazing.

I read Scott Peck's book *The Road Less Traveled*. I planned not to like the book because the snob in me could not accept that something that popular could possibly have any true merit, but it does. He speaks about grace and laziness. People are stuck in their own sadness because they are too lazy to change; and some people are, simply, blessed with grace. I believe that. It is evident from reading your letter that you have a grace inside of you that you recognize and that you are afraid to admit or afraid to speak about because you do not want to be considered better than your neighbor. It is a difficult thing to explain.

Let me try to say it differently: Your letter clearly shows that you are heading for the more difficult path in life … a life of reflection, a life lived below the surface, a life that allows you to feel and pray and touch and read and swim and love in a way that is connected to your body, your spirit, your childhood self, your adult self.

All this is confusing. The longer you live, the better you will be able to understand your struggling inner nature, and you will be able to find an outlet for the power that it gives you. Some people write, some sing, some raise a family, some join law firms, others plant roses. How we express our sensual, spiritual, and intellectual selves defines who we are.

That you have a boiling inner self is frightening, but it is also exciting and filled with hope. You are a child born into the tradition of faith. This tradition has colored your first twenty-one years with the comfort of hearing about God and heaven and hope. Now you are beginning to put that faith to a test. Actually God is beginning to whisper to you, "Liz, Liz my child, what do you think I ask of you?" We spend a lifetime trying to figure that out. Many people do not believe in God, do not believe in the question; but God opens the journey anyway.

Many people go through their lives just walking along, taking what comes, enjoying the good times, and enduring the bad. Other people along the way react, fight, embrace, struggle, love, reflect, *feel* . . . I think you are in this second group. Your "basic" struggles, as you wrote, are just as powerful and just as demanding as the struggles you read about in my book. It is the struggle, Liz, that is at the heart of what it means to be a human being. The peripheral story surrounding the struggle doesn't matter, and each story of struggle is just as different as each person. What does make you special (and I will speak about your specialness in a minute) is that you recognize that the basic struggle exists.

That you came from a comfortable upbringing, that you lived with status and power . . . these things are all circumstantial. A young woman born into poverty can have the same feeling of something special inside of her as you do . . . you might be mistaking your notion of being extraordinary with the physical beauty you have been surrounded with all your life.

Did you ever read *A Tree Grows in Brooklyn* or *My Antonia* or *The Grapes of Wrath*? These books are about extraordinary women who were poor and uneducated and who had a strength and beauty that surpassed the circumstances of their lives. You are not an extraordinary woman because of your background, Liz. You are extraordinary because you have grace; and you are allowing that grace to fill you, to worry you, to challenge you, to make you seek out answers. In many ways, you are just beginning this quest, an inescapable path because you cannot escape your nature . . . and that nature is a gift from God. Yes, your parents gave you so much. They gave you the chance to survive and grow. Roots and wings, as they say.

Please don't ever apologize for being an idealistic person. That is my biggest fault. It is why I love the play *Man of La Mancha* so much. It is what I love so much about Sydney Carton in *A Tale of Two Cities*. Both men were filled with idealism and hope, and they never gave up—never. Never give up your ideas of beauty and goodness and passion. These are hints of heaven, Liz, on this earth; and if you can find people in your life who share this vision, you will be a lucky person indeed.

Most people will not feel what you feel or recognize what you feel, for there isn't anyone just like you. But you will come across fellow pilgrims who recognize the smile and the grimace, the combined pain and glory in the eyes. That is the secret, Liz, that combination. It is in the eyes. Look deeply into the eyes of someone you love, and you will always see both glory and sadness, passion and inhibition.

You say, now, that you realize after all that you are not the best at anything. As a writer, I struggle with that all the time—*all* the time, Liz. Do you know what it is like to make an attempt at being a writer of beauty, a writer of works of art, a true writer in the reality of Charles Dickens or Mary Oliver or Harper Lee or F. Scott Fitzgerald or Loren Eiseley? I have to accept every day that I am not the best writer, or even among the best. I *once* thought that my writing was better than any other writer's.

And yet, here is the odd thing. You are right. You are not any more extraordinary than anyone else in the world . . . and yet you are. I remember my first grade teacher telling us that there will never, ever be another person like us in the entire history of the world—past, present, and future. You know this simple thing, of course. You can look at your hand and believe that the swirls at the tips of your fingers will never match anyone else's fingerprints. That is an extraordinary bit of knowledge. No one will ever be you. So we are different, and yet we are the same.

26

I love Walt Whitman's and Carl Sandburg's poetry for this notion. They speak so often about all people being one soul. Do you think Mozart felt he was special and different and extraordinary? Do you think Emily Dickinson felt special and extraordinary? Well, yes they did, but not more or less than you and I feel it to be so about ourselves. We can say, "But look at the music and poetry they created. They must have believed that they were extraordinary"... and they are because of what they created. But, Liz, they were people, ordinary people with particular gifts...overt gifts, but separate from what they were during the routine of their ordinary lives.

You are special. You are extraordinary. How you carry your unique inside self as you walk the journey of your life is what defines your grace, your dance, your beauty, your gifts, your wisdom. You say it so clearly in your wonderful letter: "What is average? Even people who seem shallow and boring and selfish often have a wealth to offer if they are encouraged with compassion and sincerity. Even those of us who seem outgoing and content and capable have a wealth of problems and questions that are not always solvable with education, organization, or social skills." Exactly. You see that with compassion and sincerity we can all blossom and discover that inner voice, that inner dignity, that inner beauty; and this does not need to come from wealth, education, or social status.

I wonder what problems you have and what deeper questions you are struggling with. You have an obvious sensitivity that, perhaps, isn't being nurtured.

I was powerfully interested in your feelings of sacrifice. Yes, love is putting yourself before others. There is a simple quote: "I am third." I like that: God, others, then self. But remember too Liz, that we are not meant to give up who we are for the love of others. Love involves a union, a mutual give-and-take, a mutual meal of grace that builds up both parties. If you give yourself and forget the self, there will be nothing left. But if you can give yourself completely to those you love and maintain who you are in the center, you give a great gift, then: your true self.

If you are meant to be the next Mother Teresa and push aside all your earthly possessions, well then, that is what you will do. But make sure that it is *your* journey, not hers. There is nothing wrong with wanting to have comfort, money, power; some of these things come to us if we are faithful to our vocations. What I find troubling is the sacrificing of ourselves for these things. You see, Liz, it also depends on how you define comfort, money, and power. I sleep in a little house, in a bed with sheets. Isn't that comfort? I have enough money to walk into a bookstore and buy any book I want. Isn't that wealth? I am a powerful person in the hearts of my children. Isn't that power enough?

I was charmed by the honesty of your letter, the frustration you feel sometimes at not being recognized. Yes, you feel you are extraordinary, and you feel people should take notice. That is a good thing. You have a powerful sense of self. Don't ever give that up.

What is your major? What do you want to do with your life? It sounds like you might be interested in some sort of service work: teacher, psychologist, foundation work with an organization of some sort. I don't know, but it seems as if you have lots to offer. Yes, we have to choose to give. It is hard to give and to give freely.

Try to give away as a gift one of your most prized possessions; it doesn't have to be something expensive but something personal and meaningful. See what it feels like when you choose to let it go. It hurts!

We have to make choices in our lives. That is partly what it means to be an adult. You see, Liz, in your letter, you are right: "The extraordinary can only appear when you are unaware of it creeping up on you." Your letter was extraordinary, and you are completely unaware of it. Yes, do not chase the extraordinary . . . let it feed you, let it cause you to blossom naturally. I try in my writing to help people see the extraordinary in the ordinary and the ordinary in the extraordinary . . . that upside-down world you wrote about.

Yes, as you wrote, we are inundated with selfishness and ambition, lust and short-term satisfaction. I thought what you wrote was eloquent: "I need glimpses into the upside-down kingdom every now and then to remind myself that not everyone lives like that, not everyone is fooled; real power is not to be found on that scale."

All you have to do is focus on being inundated with unselfishness and vocation and sensuality and long-term satisfaction. You are right; these are the glimpses in the upside-down kingdom. That you *see* this makes you extraordinary, makes you want to take the harder road in life—the road of reflection and puzzlement. You will spend your life seeking what is beautiful and good and lovely and sensual and calm and warm and restful and holy. That is counter to what many people are looking for today.

You say that you want to be a part of all that I have written and believe in. You already are, Liz, because of your vision. You already see what I see. Enclosed is one of my books for you: *Songs of Innocence and Experience.* Much of what is in that book is about you.

You are attracted to my viewpoint because it is your viewpoint, or a viewpoint of life that you are just beginning to form. Isn't that good? Isn't that wonderful that you know that you will find people along the way who will feel and understand the inside you? You will blossom. You must protect what is extraordinary about you. Self-love is important too.

I would like to ask you a favor. Your letter to me was so fine that I would like to include much of it in my book about Henri Nouwen. Let me know.

I would like to come back and talk again at North Park. Who knows?

I will also tell you this: That you acted on your impulse to write me was a good thing, a charming thing, and I am grateful for the risk you took in writing and for your belief that I would understand you and your letter. Liz, you already have a vision, you already *see.* That will be one of your burdens in life ... but it will also be one of your greatest gifts. How you use your vision is your choice. (Read Madeleine L'Engle's *A Circle of Quiet.*)

Thank you for writing. I am so very pleased that you exist.

Warmest regards,

Christopher de Vinck

Letter Three

Traveling Down a Different Path

Once you decide something, you are traveling down a different internal path than before you made that decision; so for that reason alone, it is pivotal. I think that your book about your brother Oliver was a powerful reminder for me that I can pursue things that feel right and true to me, that it does work to turn my back on the world's way of measuring success, that I can and should pursue deeper, longer lasting things.

Dear Christopher de Vinck:

I received your present in the mail Monday. I was grinning all through choir practice and called my best friend (who is also my boyfriend) right away to have him read the letter that I got from you! I know that if I ever write books that provoke readers to respond, I will take the time to write people back. It was such a great connection to be able to have such a long, personal response from an author. (It is easy to forget that authors and other figures removed from our own everyday existence are regular people too!) I appreciate the time and energy that you gave to my letter, and the personal thought and attentiveness with which you addressed the issues that I wrote about. It was like a personal book, written for me, talking about many of the topics that are my favorites to discuss! (Also, I love the few chapters that I have read so far of *Songs of Innocence and Experience*.)

Thanks again for taking the time (and for being the kind of person who does take the time) to write to me, to respond to what I was really saying, to understand the person I really am trying to become. It means a great deal to me to hear from others who are on the same journey, as you put it, to understand the inward life.

Here are some basic answers to the questions that you asked me in your response. I *am* in many ways frustrated and dealing with questions, as you perceived, but much of that has to do with where I am in the time line of my life. I have eight months (or so it seems) to decide if I want to start a job (doing what?), get further schooling (and in what subject?), do missions work (where and doing what?), pursue friendships from college (which ones and how?), and continue seriously dating or get engaged or take a break from my closest friend Peter, since we both graduate next May and are not sure how to decide where to take our relationship.

In the middle of all the practical decisions that I know need to be made, there is a still voice calling to me, reminding me that I can't let myself dilute my priorities while making these big choices. I have not really had that much practice trusting God in truly big decisions. Often I have felt that God puts me in places where the decision is obvious. There have been times when I was surprised by somewhat strange, last-minute answers; but because everything seemed right and felt right, I felt that God was speaking to me and leading me.

Right now I am feeling a blank reply from heaven. I know enough to understand that my focus shouldn't necessarily be on these choices but on the *method* that I use to get to them, but I am still restless about these seemingly blank responses.

Yes, I *am* very sensitive to things; this brings me much pain and much joy. On one hand, I am trying to make crucial decisions with the "big picture" in mind. On the other hand, I am wading through questions and not feeling really convinced one way or the other.

While I know that God can use me in many places and with many people and that I can make the most of the opportunities in life, I also realize that with each choice I make I am defining who I want to be and what is important to me.

Once you decide something, you are traveling down a different internal path than before you made that decision; so for that reason alone, it is pivotal. I think that your book about your brother Oliver was a powerful reminder for me that I can pursue things that feel right and true to me, that it does work to turn my back on the world's way of measuring success, that I can and should pursue deeper, longer lasting things. For me these might include ministry or writing or mission work. Those are the things that I am passionate about.

My majors here in college are Biblical/Theological Studies and Psychology. I have a minor in Biology (left over from a stubborn streak to prove that girls can be smart in science) that I abandoned just last year to pick up my Bible major. I love my classes this year and feel nurtured by the professors that I have. I have been rewarded for choosing the "less marketable" major.

I am tentatively exploring mission options or working with various nonprofit organizations for the year after I graduate. I've also thought about pursuing doctoral work in biblical studies (we need smart women in that field too!) or some form of ministry degree and maybe teaching at the college level. I have also thought about getting a master's degree in social work or eventually going to medical school.

I am learning that I like challenges and tend to rise to what is placed before me. If I am not challenged I get bored and wither, so I am constantly trying new things to explore where I am really challenged and what I am passionate about.

I love learning. I love people and all that they have to teach me, and I love thinking about and asking hard questions that make people uncomfortable. *I love going below the surface* more than anything. I love being outside and traveling and enjoying what nature teaches me. I also *love* all the arts (singing, piano, writing, painting, speaking), although I am not good enough at any of those things to do it as a vocation. But my vocation is what I do for fun on the weekends as much as it is what I get paid to do Monday through Friday, right? See, my idealism is shining through!

About using my letter in your book about Henri Nouwen—yes, you may! I am surprised and glad that you asked. May I see a copy of it when it is all done? I will want to read your book. I don't know much about Nouwen, but I read *Compassion* (he was one of three who wrote that book) my freshman year and loved their perspective and passion for people and God. I am honored that you want to use it.

Can you tell me, do you always include letters and writings from others in your own books or are *The Power of the Powerless* and this one on Nouwen exceptions? Also, I would love to know what process you as an author go through—from seeing a topic that you want to write about, to developing that idea, to completing a readable and significant book. Do you have a formula, or do you just respond to something that catches your attention that you can pour your creativity and soul into? Books and words are so fascinating to me. I think that recorded words help us to document life, to hold onto it longer so that we can swirl it around in our mouths, enjoying every drop before it passes by.

Thank you again for your obvious interest in what I wrote to you. I hope I am not being presumptuous by asking you more questions and telling you more about my life. I know that you probably receive lots of letters from people whose only connection to you is your books; and while I know that it is a powerful connection, I also know that you have too many of those connections to keep them all growing.

I appreciate all of your recommendations for books to read and words of wisdom regarding life in general. I have been blessed and encouraged by your reminders about how to look at myself and how to hold onto my vision. We all need those glimpses into the upside-down kingdom and the encouragement that it is okay to be on that scale. I hope in some way that you were also encouraged and spurred on by what I wrote to you. So thank you for everything.

If it is helpful at all to communicate with me via e-mail, I have an account through the university that I check at least once a week. Otherwise, best of luck in writing this new book and continuing to share your vision with others through your writing and through who you are. I am richer because of it.

Liz Mayho

Letter Four

where DO I GO from HERE?

*You hint at many possibilities for your future...
but what do you really want to do? As you sit
and pray or as you walk through the campus or
as you are awake in bed in the middle of the
night, what is it that you find yourself fighting?
What is it that you don't really want to admit
about your future? What is it that you really feel
you need to do with your life? I believe that you
already know what you want to do, but you just
haven't stood up and said yes.*

Dear Liz Maybo:

I am pleased that you accepted my book, *Songs of Innocence and Experience* as a present. It was meant to be a gift. I have made it a part of my way of being to try and do things that people don't expect—simply because I like surprises. I was coming home from dropping off my youngest son at his soccer practice and there was this sunset, all purple and red and clouds just sitting above these small mountains that protrude up beyond the western borders of the village, and it was a gift. I think God likes to drop hidden gifts to us along the way.

When you wrote your first letter it was like that sunset: unbidden, unexpected, and something more—filled with risk-taking. You were honest and real and taking a chance that the boiling inside of you wouldn't spill out too much, and yet you were so filled with something to say. I felt grateful that I was the recipient of your churning, inside, sunset self. So nice to think of you smiling in choir practice because of something that arrived all the way from New Jersey.

I am glad that you shared my letter with your best friend, Peter. I am dedicating my book on Henri to my best friend, my wife. It will read: "To Roe: my partner in the journey." I cannot write to everyone the way I write to you for I just don't have the time. But there are, now and again, letters that arrive, people who step into my life, and I feel, for whatever reason, that there ought to be more between us. We extend ourselves in this world so rarely in ways that are truly significant. Your first letter was significant. I wanted to honor that, and you.

37

I too like to discuss the topics that are your favorites. You have a searching heart, and that is good. It reminds me of me many years ago; though I must admit that I was a late bloomer. It wasn't until I was 34 that I really began to understand the hidden way. I am also interested in seeing who you will become. You say you are trying to become someone. You have so much already...but now what to do with the gift of you? That is the struggle. You are lucky. You ask the question. The search for the inner life or for a way to that inner life or for a way to making that inner life more public or more revealing takes risk. I think that I wrote last time about vulnerability. To open your inner self to others demands vulnerability, and that is frightening sometimes.

Where do you want to move the elephant? That is what you are asking yourself at this time in your life. Yes, you are nearly finished with another part of your life, and such an end is asking you the elephant question. Place the elephant in the circus or by the river or in the fields or in the sight of a rifle or in a herd, what? Each question is filled with traps, puzzlements, and consequences. For me those questions were easy. I liked people and I liked books, so I became a teacher. I became a writer many years later and by accident. But of course I now see it was by design, not my design, but a design just the same.

It is obvious from the very little I know about you that you have many talents—gifts, really. You have been graced with intellectual gifts...and your aversion to boredom prods the elephant. I often suggest to my seniors in high school a way to think about their future. I ask them to think back to any moment in any class or in any situation in the last four years that brought them a significant jolt in their inside world. Perhaps it was something a teacher said in chemistry; perhaps it was a historical moment, a mathematical equation, a scientific experiment, a day in the nursing home, a book, or a poem. I ask the students to identify something like that, then I tell them that that moment is a clear hint as to what they might want to pursue in their lives.

Liz, think about the past four years. What brought you closest to yourself or what brought you an inside soul-jolt where you said to yourself, "Hey that was neat!" That moment, in my mind, is a clear starting point for a career and a future.

If, in your studies of biology, you found a part of your passion and joy and something special mixed in with the bone structure of a cat, well, there is a career: medicine. If you felt a strong pull in your mission work, and I mean a dragging pull, well then, pursue that.

I worry about mission work that is connected to a college experience where it is like a study abroad, and you know there is a time when you can go home. Mission work means, to me, that you can never go home again, for your home is with those you serve. Someone who arrives, does good work, and leaves is not a true missionary. A missionary arrives, grabs a hammer, and builds his or her own house. That is not to say that you cannot do mission work all your life right in your own town, right in your own church, right in your own neighborhood. How far do you think you would have to go until you found someone who needs your words of hope? I'd say probably no farther than four doors down from your house.

You ask yourself if you want to pursue your friendships from college. That will decide itself. People stay in touch or they don't. Whom do you love as friends? Whom do you really love and want to make a lifetime commitment to, as a friend? These kind of friendships go beyond just having college experiences in common. That is a dangerous question, almost as dangerous as the marriage question, because real love takes time and effort. We cannot extend our vulnerable selves to too many people. It would exhaust us.

And there is Peter. I wonder how much of your turmoil involves Peter. Do you love him? Do you feel nurtured by him? Do you see his flaws? Does he see your flaws? Does he cherish you? Does he speak about inside things? Does he make you laugh? Do you feel the vocation of marriage pulling you toward him? I think that if you have suspicions that these answers are not coming from the woman inside of you, then you are still in need of building a bridge between yourself and Peter. If the child and the adult in you are blending nicely with Peter, if the thought of spending a lifetime with Peter changes the color of your cheeks, well, then, I would suggest that you move forward with him.

How do you know if the person you are thinking about marrying is the person you can promise to be together with for the rest of your life? I am always interested in the idea of arranged marriages that worked: strangers meeting strangers, together for a lifetime, making a go of it admirably. There is a wonderful collection of photographs called *The Family of Man* that you might want to find. One section is called, I think, "We Two Form a Multitude." I like that notion of two people joining together, forming a sense of unity. Where do you want to move the elephant?

Do you ever worry that you spend too much energy thinking about things? To be a reflective person, as you obviously are, seems to demand a troubled heart. We are always asking ourselves small and large questions. Often there are no answers, no this-way or that-way answers . . . just movement in a direction that has its own consequences and surprises. Of course, you haven't had to trust in God for truly big decisions yet. Now is the time to consider that voice inside of you that is God's voice nudging you a bit. Because we are given free will, we have choices. But don't you think God offers gentle guidance along the way ?

That you are feeling a blank reply from heaven startles me because you believe heaven gives answers. It is good to hear that young people still believe in the voices from heaven. Liz, we cannot do it all. You will be dazzled for all of your life with possibilities . . . and most of those possibilities you will not be able to pursue simply because you cannot do all that you wish, travel everywhere, pursue all relationships, do different careers. You will find yourself involved with certain routines, certain relationships, certain careers; and if you are wise and open to God's vision, if you are graced, those routines and relationships and careers will be enough to sustain you and protect you from being too diffused and watered down in the spirit and in the body.

That my books help you simply to trust how you feel deep inside, well, that is a victory for me. What are those deeper, long-lasting things, Liz? That is exactly the question you are writing. That you know what you are passionate about is already giving you a sense of direction.

We spend our lives both trying to return to our mothers and fathers and trying to move forward into God's arms. Someday, if you have children, you will know the smell of a baby's breath deep in the middle of the night. There at that moment you will know the bridge between the long-ago past and the long-into-the-future place where you cannot go. We send the message of hope forward each time we fall in love, each time we shake someone's hand, each time a child is born, each time the day ends with a prayer.

I like so much to hear about your stubborn streak to prove that girls can be smart in science. You are fortunate to be born into a world that is much more open to women. (Though on a global level, I fear that women are as vulnerable as they were thirty years ago.) Women in the United States have more power and freedom to pursue who they are.

You mention the possibility of medical school. You said this last, and I wonder if this is what is at the center of your puzzlement. Sometimes what we mention last is really what we want to mention first, but we are afraid to admit it. You speak about the possibility of mission work or getting involved in a nonprofit organization or pursuing a doctorate in biblical studies or pursuing a ministry degree or teaching in a college. Whatever you do, remember that the center of you, the variety of your passions, will be fulfilled. I have centered my life around my family and my writing and my career in education. All these things tend to my passions. Do I wish I pursued a career in journalism? Sometimes. Did I consider being a priest once? Yes. Have I met women who attracted me? Of course. But twenty-two years later I find myself still married to the same woman whom I still love. We have three children. I am still working in education. I still write. It seems to me that we end up doing God's work eventually without even realizing it.

You hint at many possibilities for your future ... but what do you *really* want to do? As you sit and pray or as you walk through the campus or as you are awake in bed in the middle of the night, what is it that you find yourself fighting? What is it that you don't really want to admit about your future? What is it that you really feel you need to do with your life? I believe that you already know what you want to do, but you just haven't stood up and said yes. Do not fear the answer yes. You will know when you make a right decision because of an open, stepping-into-it feeling.

You like challenges. Good. I challenge you to write back about what is deepest in your heart about your future, about what you want in a career and in a relationship. I also like that you are not afraid to ask people hard questions that make them uncomfortable. You love going below the surface. So I offer you this: Ask me hard questions. Dare to go below the surface with this suddenly new stranger who has come into your life. Also, what do you like to do for fun ... I mean *real* fun?

Thank you for allowing me to use your letter in my book. It is now included, and the book is finished. It is with the editor; and in a few months I will receive the proofs, and I will send a copy along to you so that you can see how I used your letter and read the rest of the book. I think you will be pleased.

No, I don't use letters in most of my books. *The Power of the Powerless* was my first book where I used letters. Your first letter to me arrived while I was working on the last quarter of the book, as I was also working on the introduction and conclusion. Then when I read your letter, it simply fit exactly what I was working on. The book is about the journey we are all on and how we tend to that journey. You are at the beginning of that journey, you are so articulate, and you sounded so charming and bright; well, your letter fit. You will see.

Much of my life has been serendipitous. Your coming into my life follows that same pattern. I will tell you this early on: all, and I mean all, of the most wonderful things in my life have come to me unbidden...gifts from God, really, and at just the right time. Think about this, Liz: There are people in this world whom you have not yet met but who will have a profound impact on your life. Isn't that exciting to think there are so many people who are just waiting for you?

Your asking about how I go about writing already shows that, as you say, you like to ask questions. I like that about you. (How else do we get below the surface without asking questions?) With Oliver's book I came to it out of necessity. When I wrote the original essay for *The Wall Street Journal*, I had no idea that that little piece would have an impact on so many people. And after I received those extraordinary letters, I just felt compelled to do something with it all.

I was reading at the time Russell Baker's autobiography (I forget the name of it). He began his book with the death of his mother. I found that to be significant, so I began my book about death and about our perceptions of death. From writing that book I came to my own realization that how we look at death determines how we look at life. Simple. So I wrote Oliver's book, keeping my eye closely on the theme: the power of the powerless. It was easy to put together once I had that central idea.

Most of my books are just collections of my essays. The way I write an essay: I receive quite a bit of mail, which means that my desk usually has open envelopes scattered here and there. I will think of an experience that I had and jot that down in one sentence. Then I will try and think of another experience, book, or idea that is related in any way to that first story I thought about. When you have two things that are similar, for whatever reason, you can begin to determine more specifically what makes those things similar. Or, as they say in writing classes: A theme begins to emerge. It is the same thing with scientific data—we gather data to draw conclusions. I look at an experience, think about something else that is related, and suddenly there is a theory, a notion about life. Then I write the essay. As I write the essay, things come to me that fit the overall composition—these things come from all the reading and living and seeing I've done. I cannot teach anyone how to write because writing ability comes from a reading, living experience.

I can tell you this: It is a wonderful thing to be writing and to have something that fits so well pop into my mind. Some people say these things pop into our heads because our mind is built to make connections among data that we store. I like to think that this connecting ability is God's hinting, God's helping. This is, in a small way, how I go about my writing.

When I write poetry I always listen to music. When I write prose, I do not. I could go on at great length about the writing of poetry, but it comes down to the same method: reading, reading, reading. Poetry is music in many ways. I do not have a formula, but if you look at all of my books as a whole, you will see that, yes, I am talking about many of the same things over and over again: loneliness, childhood memories, sex, education, marriage, old age, my children, a fondness for what was done in my youth. If you want to know about my writing style, simply read some books by Loren Eiseley. It is from his work that I learned about the power of mingling sadness with beauty. I have written about this in my books: I strive for a tone of voice in my work that is both beautiful and sad.

I write about the past in first person with a mood of reflection, regret, and joy. It is a difficult thing to see such beauty in the world and know there is such pain. That is what I try to do. I, like you, am an idealist. I write because I am alone. (And I am surrounded with my wife and children and students and my parents and brothers and sisters. It has nothing to do with them or with my relationship with them.) And you are also right: Words help us to swirl life around in our mouths, enjoying every drop and tasting the mixture.

I am pleased about your presumptions by asking me more questions and telling me more about your life. I hope that you ask more questions and that you continue to tell me more about yourself. And yes, I do receive a fair number of letters from people who read my books. In truth, I answer them all, trying to return something significant. I have the ability to return a kindness to people who write to me, but I cannot get involved in an extended correspondence with every person who writes to me. It would exhaust me, and I don't have the time; so please understand that my writing to you is something I very much *want* to do. Your letters are beyond the typical, kind letters that I receive; and I want to give you the time that I can because I feel *compelled* to do so. (I added that word to my storage bank because you used it in your first letter.) You are right, Liz, we all need glimpses into the upside-down kingdom and the encouragement that it is OK to be on that scale. Your letter added to my encouragement.

I don't want to correspond with you through e-mail for a very good reason. I find e-mail to be too easy, and I am susceptible to just dash off a few lines that "takes care of" the "obligation" of writing, and I lose the opportunity to write something significant. When I receive an e-mail I feel compelled to answer it and move on, much like a message on the phone. We are losing each second the art or the impetus to have real correspondences with people. Something too: I like so much receiving mail and having the actual letter and signature of the person who writes. E-mail is so blank-looking with no signature, no feel for the paper or card chosen, no smell of ink. Also, a letter can linger on my desk for days or weeks before I answer it, and I feel comfortable with this because it allows me to write back when I have comfortable time and when I can focus specially on the person I am writing to. But I will give you my e-mail address just in case you need or want to write quickly for any particular reason.

What is your full name? Elizabeth?

Warmest regards,

Christopher de Vinck

Letter Five

contentment and passion

I know that I am young and that I have many options and much time, but I feel as if I don't want to waste time or people or opportunities that I encounter. It is a fine line for me to walk: to passionately live out all the things that I see as being vital on the one hand and yet to be content and not always wanting more on the other. How do you push and strive toward the future, but not miss the present?

Dear Christopher:

May I use your first name? It sounds too formal to write your
full name every time. What would you prefer? And yes, my
full name is Elizabeth, although only my family calls me that
(or Beth). Family friends who watched me grow up still call
me Lizzy or Bethie, and my brother still calls me Na. (As a
baby he couldn't pronounce the "z," and somehow he ended
up with "Na.")

This is my reward to myself tonight, to write to you about
myself and my life and what I thought about after your letter
arrived. I am in a time crunch that will last until the beginning of December when we have our Christmas break. I have
roughly 120 pages (in theory) to write for various classes, and
only, let's see, five weeks to get it all done. I always struggle
with big deadlines and homework assignments because 1) I
am fairly good at flying by the seat of my pants and don't like
to plan ahead much; 2) I am fairly smart and usually can get
away with doing # 1; and 3) I don't stress that much about
grades anyway, because in the end, my report card and
resume are not the most important things to me. My life and
other people's lives are, however, and both of those tend to
rush right by when I am in hot pursuit of things like grades or
things that this world measures us by. That being true, I
understand that I do need to "apply myself" and appreciate
the money and time my parents and I are investing in this
school. Overall, the point of college is to learn and go to
classes. I struggle with it all though, because honestly, I feel
that I learn more from relationships, from small group Bible

studies and chapel services, from working at Urban Outreach (our service organization, known as UO), from volunteering, from living with others in a dorm, from driving home over breaks with them, from going out for coffee, or from singing in a concert than I ever do in a classroom. I almost see the classroom as the place to rest and test out my theories about how life really works. I guess that's kind of backwards from the way it is supposed to work! So I made myself finish a paper tonight (a Friday night!) before I would let myself write to you. I have learned that linking my homework to people motivates me. "If I get my work done early, then I will have time to be with others or to be available when they may need me in the future." Rationale like that works pretty well for me.

You asked me some wonderful questions that gave my mind fuel and encouragement to work. Thank you for those things! It is rare, actually, that I feel like someone is really able to challenge me. Not that I am so terrific; it's just that I am on a different wavelength and usually don't say 80 percent of what I am thinking because I don't believe others would really care about it. I know I have met a kindred spirit when I read or hear someone's words, and these words resonate deep inside me.

I am breathing in the soothing, spicy smell of a burning candle and watching the flame's shadow dance on the wall; I just bought the soundtrack to the movie *Shine*, and I have that playing on repeat, filling my room with beautiful piano harmonies and some orchestral arrangements as well. That should give you the flavor of my personality even more. This is one of my most relaxing places to be. *Mmmmmm...*

There were some very specific things that your letter evoked in me, so I am going to address those first. Your comments about how to know what to do with my career were insightful. I agree that mission work should not be a haphazard, short-term endeavor. I have always felt some kind of "call" (the only word I can think of to explain this feeling) to do mission work, and I try to do that in some way every day. Not to cross it off from my "to do" list, but because I get so much out of it and feel like that is where I find the real stuff of life.

Part of my drive to go somewhere else (i.e., on a mission trip) is, I think, a mild form of denial, of running away from things that are here and that seem set, formidable, and limiting. I want to break free and rebel—never in huge, detrimental ways and rarely because I am actually oppressed. But I have observed myself thinking this way. Of course, that is the exact opposite reason that one should have for doing mission work; I wouldn't serve others and make big decisions based on a rebellious attitude.

I often feel a tension between the knowledge of what I *should* do and the self-realization that I don't *want* to do it. I am disgusted when I do things that are not genuine, and yet, let's face it—there will always be days when I do not want to be kind or gentle or to listen to others. And yet, I should probably still do those things; and sometimes doing the action does indeed make those things more a genuine part of me.

I felt too much rebellion behind my reasoning in pursuing medical school. The wrong reasons were driving me there, and it felt wonderful to finally switch my majors and absorb information that I loved and actually wanted to know for my personal use. I still love the study of the body and all the wonder and magic that it holds and the ability to help others that a medical skill gives. I have not distinguished yet where that belongs in my life, though. Medical school would be a huge time and energy commitment, and knowing my tendency to put academic learning behind "life" learning, I may not be the best candidate! I was impressed that you picked up on my penchant for that field, however.

About the feeling you spoke of, the stirring that says that something is important and that is what life is really about, let me say that I am so glad that you did not spout the usual, practical "examine your gifts and your options and find the best combination that would yield a quality, economically stable job" response. I have heard that enough. This kind of ties into your question about what do I like to do for fun.

You asked what I like to do for real fun, the best, not just the "secondary" fun things. I get those kind of feelings when I am talking with people about their lives or God or questions or their families or weird theories about the universe. I thrive on deep conversations (this is one of the primary reasons that Peter and I have been dating for so long).

I love helping people. Volunteer work is really, really fun for me, as is my administrative job at UO. I plan all our programs and teach a staff of students how to lead other students to volunteer. I love seeing them learn and get excited and hearing all the ideas that they can create and pursue. I think leaders and teachers and parents end up learning more from those that they are leading, teaching, and parenting, don't you? I mean more of the *important* things. Sometimes I think that positions of authority dilute our thinking and our vision, and only children or young students or those who haven't volunteered before can remind us of our original reasons for doing them.

I also love music and writing. Hearing certain music, usually classical favorites involving piano and strings, or reading beautiful lyrics or quotes (and sometimes poetry) affect me greatly. I talk about all of those things for days after I experience them.

I love house plans too! Architecture has been my hobby since I was about eight years old. I collected house plans, decorating techniques, environmentally friendly building articles, kitchen planners, and I took drafting for two years in high school. It seems unrelated to all of my passions though, so for the time being that one is only a pastime.

I love traveling and nature and the beauty of the physical world. I especially love the mountains in Colorado. I think that I could be happily employed pumping gas at a station in the middle of Estes Park for a lifetime, if there were interesting people and spiritual support around. I am pulled toward the mountains. Don't I sound like a huge sap? I suppose I am in a lot of ways!

Other things that I do for real fun? Taking pictures, playing with children, doing creative things, being alone and relaxing, swing dancing, sending people cards and letters I have made, walking outside at night alone, listening, laughing, and just being myself with people, being with friends on a road trip, biking, singing the harmony on a great song, arranging piano and guitar pieces, discovering new little nooks in Chicago that become "one of my spots," curling up in front of the fireplace at home with a blanket and a hot drink and music so loud you have to turn the lights off and swim in it, watching funny or dramatic movies, staying up late talking with my dad and my friends about theology and life and big issues, talking about everything honestly with Peter, or doing just about anything with my younger brother, Tim. I definitely need both alone time and time to be with other people, to be active and then to be relaxed.

There is also the practical, more administrative side of me. I love improving systems and places and patterns, whether it is through organizing them or being more efficient or focusing more on people instead of the process itself. I was given so much freedom in my job at UO that I was able to change many things and help out in ways that will last after I leave. I love feeling that I strategically improved something for others in the future. I like planning ahead in that sense, I suppose. I like having freedom and being my own authority. That rebel part of me isn't so fond of obeying rules just to obey them, although I really do believe that often they save many others from being hurt in the long run. That is how I can make myself follow rules—if I see them connecting to people, so that they are linked with what I think is important.

This summer I worked with middle-school students back in Minnesota, and my job was to take them on service trips around the city. I was able to be outside and with people all day (teenagers are really fun) and do different things all the time through leading the group (but being taught by them too). I got to see the change in their lives as, over two weeks, they became compassionate toward a brain-damaged client, stopped throwing their garbage on the sidewalk, and were kinder and more understanding even to one another. All of those things excite me because hopefully these middle-school students will continue to learn and grow from their experiences this summer and impact others through their lives with service, helping people their own age become more involved and sensitive as well. I easily become fired up about those kinds of things: dealing with people and the future.

I also love understanding and learning. I love that feeling of bringing together things from different aspects of life and coming up with a cohesive solution, whatever the situation may be.

What to do with all those thoughts and questions that do not have many answers? I think it is slowly unraveling, but for now it gives my mind more to mull and muse over. Yes, I worry that I spend too much energy thinking. I am miserable when I am fake, however; so I have to think things through and can't just ignore issues running through my brain. I like being goofy and relaxed, and I love laughing, but not if I am in a serious mood or if someone else is upset or if there are other things going on below the surface and people just want to be goofy to cover up reality. I suppose this can be a form of therapy for other people, but it is draining for me. (Consequently, I am also a terrible liar!)

What I will do next year is up for grabs. Maybe short-term missions, here or overseas, maybe working with COOL (Campus Outreach Opportunity League), or helping plan more college groups. I know that I want to attend graduate school in the not-too-distant future, and I feel like social work (getting a MSW) might be the place for me or maybe seminary. I have enjoyed my biblical/theology classes so much that I feel guilty receiving credit and grades for them! I would read and write about these topics on my own, anyway. I know that I am young and that I have many options and much time, but I feel as if I don't want to waste time or people or opportunities that I encounter. It is a fine line for me to walk: to be passionate and live out all the things that I see as being vital on the one hand and yet to be content and not always wanting more on the other. How do you push and strive toward the future, but not miss the present? I think that I struggle with that a lot.

You wondered how much of my turmoil involves Peter. Well, quite a lot and then not so much — all at the same time. He is the most understanding, loving, thoughtful, intelligent, challenging, honest, deep friend that I have ever had (and I have had the privilege of having many deep friendships). He tops them all, mainly for two reasons: He loves me a *lot*, and I know that; and he is perceptive and reads people and the world at a profound level. I love how he sees people and reality and deals with things as they *are* and as they *should* be, not as everyone *pretends* that they are. He is a great listener and supporter, and he keeps me grounded. We have been very close friends for three years, dating for two; so we know each other pretty well.

Yes, we know each other's weaknesses and often bring them up for discussion or improvement. He is very nurturing and cherishes me in many ways. He speaks of inside things (that's just the way he sees life), but I sometimes have to encourage him to talk (that is fairly common with guys, though!). We do not sleep together, although we are intimate after two years of intense dating. No, I do not feel marriage pulling me toward him; and that is where the problem originates. He lessens my turmoil because I am able to be completely myself with him. He can read me and my unusual thoughts and emotional turns and handle it all. Yet he is also the one person who brings me the most questioning because of how intertwined we are and because I am unsure of where it is all headed.

I have a hard time reconciling the *reality* of marriage with what I *always thought* it would be. There are days when I feel deeply committed to Peter; and I feel as if I want to marry him, but I don't trust my feelings because they go up and down and are based on who knows what. He is a little more ready to be committed than I am, but I think that reflects more his personality and the way that he can make choices versus my inability to make choices. I am always asking questions of myself and of others.

Peter is not the kind of person that I thought I would marry, or even date actually, and we have always been a little uneven that way. He started liking me as more than a friend much sooner than I liked him in that way. He practically talked me into dating him! It took me awhile to acknowledge how I felt about him and how I loved him. It also took me a while to want to work on that love and to grow in that love.

I know that love is a decision in many ways. I know that there are probably several people who would work out for me and even be good to marry; and I know that feelings need to be there, but that they still come and go. I don't want to make the decision of who I am going to be with for the rest of my life without a definitive "this is the one" from God. What form would that affirmation take, I wonder?

I am in a period of waiting while I learn to love Peter, as I think this is where I should be for now. It gets a little tricky when I think about how much I have invested in him and vice versa. I know that the more you are immersed in something the harder it is to see other options; but, if all along you look for other options, you might miss what you already have.

We have already talked about next year and how we are going to, for now, pursue our own things and not try to make them coincide with the other person's dreams. It meant a great deal to me that he was secure enough with our relationship to say that I could go and do whatever I wanted and not feel tied to him if I wasn't ready to be, and that he would do the same.

I feel that if our relationship is supposed to work out, it will happen (although what *supposed to* really means is a whole other dilemma). We can go our own ways and still love each other and work on our relationship for now. I know that I care about him, but I am not so knocked over by him that I can't imagine us not ending up together. Although, I don't know if I would ever feel that way about anyone. Several close friends of mine have said that they don't think that I will ever "be sure" or be astoundingly impressed with someone because I don't feel that way often. I don't know if you wanted that much information regarding all your questions, but that pretty much sums up where Peter and I are right now. And yes, all of that causes me intermittent turmoil in my life.

I guess I have saved for last the truly big question that I think about, and I will go into more detail in another correspondence. This letter is getting long and you already have much information to digest from my end! The issue of my relationship with God and how that fits into humanity's relationship to God, in general, takes up most of the neurons in my head. It really arcs over every other issue in life and is the sustenance for everything. Yet, just thinking about God in the theological sense does not have to affect my life. But I truly want it to affect me.

Tell me something...what do you feel like God is teaching you in this arena? How does God teach you? Do you feel as if you pursue God, or is it the other way around? Do you think that scholarship and faith have a natural communion with each other, or does one water down the other? What do you see as the strong points and the weak points of being a Catholic? Have you ever been involved with another belief practice? I finished reading *Songs of Innocence and Experience* about two weeks after you sent it to me. Your essays were my bedtime reading, perfect subjects to relax me, to make me smile, to think about just as I dozed off. Anyway, it seemed from your book that you are Catholic, but I wasn't sure. We had the Cardinal from Chicago perform mass here at North Park just last week. It was a big deal I think, from all the media coverage and publicity around town. I went and really enjoyed myself, although I was pretty confused and had to have a professor who sat next to me interpret a lot of what was going on and the reasons for it all. I had only been to one other mass.

What kind of books do you read? It sounds as if you are primarily a fiction reader. I rarely read fiction, and Peter and my other close friend Linnea bug me that I need to read more fiction. I rely on being able to see and read below the surface, but I don't want to miss anything in a book where I can't be sure that I am picking up the whole message.

How do you teach your children the kinds of things that you write about and think about? Do you talk to them about it or live it out? Do your ideas translate easily into parenting or not? How do you challenge Roe with being deep and being concerned with the upside-down kingdom's scale while still letting her be her own person? What do you like to do for *real* fun? How do you think about the choices that you had at one time but are now gone? Do you ever regret things and get caught up in thinking about the past, or do you really feel that God makes the best out of whatever you do and uses you wherever you are? How much do you think our own decisions matter, and how much do you think that we end up doing God's will anyway? Do you think God gives us faith, grace, belief?

I am intrigued with the verses in the Bible that speak about God's giving us everything that we are and have, including our own faith. That seems backwards compared to what I often hear from secular speakers. What would you say is the most important truth that you have learned that accentuates your growing in a relationship with God? with your wife? with your children? with friends? Why do you think I use the word *compelled* a lot? (I accept your challenge to ask hard questions of you with a smile and with thoughtfulness.)

One activity that I can directly connect with getting your letters is my increased desire to write. I have written poems and letters to myself, more letters to other people, more thoughts and questions and quandaries about life since you wrote me. I wrote an entire page of run-on questions that I turned in to our unofficial college poetry publication. It seems to help me to write when I feel "compelled" to do so. It helps me organize and release the pent-up thoughts and feelings that otherwise would swirl around in my mind.

Thank you for sharing more of yourself and your writing with me. I have an advantage in getting to know you since I have read two books by you that were largely autobiographical. I hope that you know how much I appreciate your letters and desire to take time to correspond with me. It is a delight! Words are *so* important.

Have a wonderful day.

Your friend,
Liz Mosbo

Letter Six

confidence
and a
pure Heart

*No, do not examine your gifts and options and
find the best combination that would yield a
quality, economically stable job. Examine your
passions and pray and light your candles. In
many ways it doesn't matter what you choose,
what matters is how you are going to love.*

Dear Liz:

I was wondering at what point you would call me Christopher. Actually, I am grateful for your quick acceptance of this new friendship. I didn't want to ask what you might call me for I didn't want to be presumptuous ... actually, I didn't want to overwhelm you. One of my weak points is that I trust too quickly, care too quickly, am open too quickly—which can lead to heartache sometimes. Having a strong personality sometimes turns people away.

My strength is not what I consider typical, in that I am quickly taken in by new people who come into my life unbidden and seem to have such gifts of personality. Then I dive right into a relationship with tenderness and gratitude. It is obvious you have such gifts, and it is obvious that I am already grateful for *your* interest in me, in my work, in my life. (Actually, I found myself looking extra carefully at the mailbox these past few days, hoping that you would write back.) And from what I already see, this letter is going to take me a few days; I am just responding to your first sentence, and I am already a quarter of the way down this first page.

Yes, call me Christopher. I have always been happy with my name. Most people call me Chris, but I always like the feeling of being called Christopher. Difficult to explain ... like the abbreviation of the state Vermont (VT). I like the word *Vermont*, and I prefer seeing the entire word spelled out. (I like that *Vermont* means "green mountains." When I discovered that I felt so smart. And when I learned that the flower-weed, *dandelion*, means in French, "the teeth of the lion," I laughed.)

Unrelated, though connected, I just finished reading an article in *The New Yorker* magazine written by John Lahr, Bert Lahr's son. Bert Lahr played the Cowardly Lion in the film version of *The Wizard of Oz*. It seems that Bert Lahr was a distant sort of man who was immersed in his desk work and acting. I liked how, in the article, it said that one of the few things that gave Lahr an honest smile was watching the "Munchkins" work during the various scenes in the making of the movie.

Before I forget, I wanted to say a bit more about your letters. I have discovered many places in my life where I have that sort of Bert Lahr smile. There are pockets, Liz, in our lives, little oases that help us on the way during our journeys. I have discovered my friendships are like those small, lush, hidden places along the way. That is how I felt when I sat on the couch and read your letter, stopping by the woods on a snowy evening. We build around us pools of joy that we can fall into and swim when we are hot or tired or thirsty or when we feel that we just want to be young again and laugh. I laughed aloud when I wrote this, just knowing how young you are!

I am glad that your full name is Elizabeth. That is my daughter's middle name. Do you ever think about what you would name your own children? Do you ever think about having your own children? What do young women your age think about these days?

I like your concept of rewards: finish this task so that I can write a letter. Giving small rewards along the way is a good suggestion. Did you ever read *To Kill a Mockingbird*? (My favorite book. I'll tell you about the type of reading I do later in this letter in response to one of your many wonderful questions.) Atticus, the father, insists that Jem, the son, read to old Mrs. Dubose each day as punishment for destroying some flowers in his neighbor's yard. Turns out she was slowly dying and was addicted to morphine. She wanted to die free of the drug, so each day that Jem came to read, she asked him to read just a bit longer. He didn't know that the longer he read, the longer she went without the morphine. Eventually she was free, and then she died. Mrs. Dubose's reward was her own dignity. She just listened and listened to the boy reading. And during the reading she suffered and waited and suffered, but each day she put off taking the drug just a bit longer. If you want to know all there is to know about compassion and raising children and justice and the power of the narrative voice, read this book.

Do you know that you have much confidence in who you are? Such confidence is one of the conditions, I believe, for a purity of heart. God gave us certain attributes. You are smart; you can succeed by zooming to keep up. I like it that you are not much of a planning person. I hardly plan anything. Most of the time I do what I feel is best to do at the moment. That works. I too feel that we learn more from relationships than from book work, but I found for myself that it is not so much the book work but reading that has changed my life.

The only advice my father gave me when I walked out the door heading for my first day in college was, "Don't let school interfere with your education." My father is a brilliant man. He knows Greek and Latin and French. He wrote books, built sailboats without any power tools, designed houses, built weaving looms. He was a college professor, an editor, a translator. He is eighty-seven and lives in the same house he and my mother bought in 1948.

I was a reserved, quiet boy when I was growing up. I remember walking to school and saying to myself, "Let's see if I can go through the whole day without someone saying a word to me." And of course no one did, and I walked home with a review of the day, "Yep. I did it. No one even said hi." In truth, outside of my family, I knew no one until I was a junior in high school. I was a lonely boy. All I knew was my family and the wonderful Polish family to the right. My life was my brothers and sisters and Maria and Johnny next door where the onion grass stained our pants in the summer, and we called out to one another across snow-covered fields in winter asking if the ice was ready for skating. Many people look back to childhood with a clouded, misty vision of nostalgia, taking from their memory only what was good. I know with certitude, Liz, that I lived in a paradise as a child that was filled with adventures in the tree fort with my brother Bruno and a small electric light that had three colors: blue, red, and green. I remember the feeling of great fancy as Anne and I built a circus in the attic. Our house was huge with long hallways and curved wood banisters. The voice of my grandmother still swirls in the kitchen of my memory. The coats hung behind the basement door, old coats that looked like camel backs and worn blankets.

That you feel challenged by my letters or that what I ask gives you reason to stop and give yourself to some inside reflection is good. I think we all need to exercise our ability to conjure up a magical self now and again. I found it interesting that you don't say as much as you think. People would probably think you were a lunatic if you did. I find myself slipping sometimes. I gave a talk in Monticello, New York, a few weeks ago, and one of the women on the hosting team had such extraordinary eyes. They were beautiful. And that is the first thing I said to her: "You have beautiful eyes." She was startled a bit, and then she gave this beautiful smile. I find that I live an inside life that never stops looking, admiring, judging, feeling. It can't be turned off, except in sleep. (But even in sleep there is wonder. Ever dream that you are flying?) I suppose, if there is a theme to this letter, it is that, yes, Liz, I too feel that you are familiar with the territory of my own fields of hope and beauty and sadness and mystery. What surprises me is that you have already stepped into the land of the upside-down kingdom at such an early age.

Thank you for writing about the candle in your room and the smell of wax and the shadows. See? Your room is one of those oases I spoke about. Such a small detail in your letter also tells me much about your passions. We live with language, and language at best gives only a hint of reality. We live with metaphors. Through the juxtaposition of image and feeling, there is meaning. Burning wax and shadows in Illinois.

You are alive and young and anxious for the future. No wonder you feel the inside need to rebel. Mission work, as I said, can be accomplished in your own neighborhood. You do not have to go to a developing nation or to the inner city to discover a need for your healing words. You have in your hands the ability to heal.

What your hands touch will turn to God's gold. Again, you just have to decide where your garden will be. I think your grace will bundle up your energy and your various interests and move you forward into a career that startles you. Do not be afraid. You will find your way. We all do, Liz. Whatever you decide to do will be easy in many ways, once you decide.

I have had various experiences in my life when I fought God's plan for me, and that struggle placed me in near-depression. Each time, however, when I said yes to the path that was obvious, the pain and doubt were lifted. An odd sensation.

I will also return to the notion of God's will that you asked about in your letter. Something I know for sure: Whatever you decide to do with your life will involve a small death inside of you, a giving over to something that was not there before and a leaving behind something that was once there. And when you do make a decision, you can't turn back. Of course you can change jobs, choices, etc. That is not what I mean. But once you select what is most significant in your life, you walk away from less significant things, which makes you stronger but also makes you less of a child.

You have to give up the ways of a child in order to return to purity of heart. Whatever your vocation eventually becomes, it will consume you. You have an obligation to have an extraordinary life. So be a doctor or a missionary or an architect or a social worker—it doesn't matter what you choose. It is obvious to me that you are surrounding yourself with options that contain many people, that you'll be doing something for many people.

As a woman you will see more and more how much people will want from you—as a mother and wife and friend—and then as whatever you choose for your profession. You will live all your life between your generous heart and your need for self-preservation. It is a battle many people fight daily. Take out one of your favorite CDs, classical preferably, play it, and listen to what your heart says. Go down a list of options as you hear the music piercing you. What leaps out? What hits you in a certain way? What do you hear?

A student stepped into my office today and announced, "Dr. de Vinck, I am going to major in international marketing." I asked Christine how she came to this decision. "I finally went to a palm reader, and she saw France in my future!"

I like your humor and your annoyance at cliché thoughts. No, do not examine your gifts and options and find the best combination that would yield a quality, economically stable job. Examine your passions and pray and light your candles. In many ways it doesn't matter what you choose, what matters is how you are going to love.

From your "fun" list I would say that you have already created in your life a fine understanding of the word *balance*. Your *thinking* fun and your *doing* fun seem well matched. A life given over to too much thinking is a life closed to people. You like conversations about life and God. That is good. God probably likes that, but I wouldn't spend *too* much time discussing life, especially in an intellectual way.

We now have a doctor in the news who injects someone with chemicals so that the person can die and be free from suffering. The nation is trying to sort out the meaning of such an act. Oliver might have been injected with death to save him from his suffering. There was a newspaper article last week about twenty or thirty people who were sentenced to the death penalty and were later, many years later, found to be innocent. Thousands of babies are born each day in this country, and we do not celebrate that reality on a national level. But give a doctor a needle filled with death, and we all look closely and nod our heads in heavy intellectual puzzlement. I say live life as an act of faith, and don't intellectualize the puzzlements along the way.

But I digress from your letter, and I fear that I am being too pedantic with you. Please be annoyed if I am annoying with my advice and thoughts.

I am glad that you love music. As you might know from reading my books, Aaron Copland is my favorite composer, above even the classical writers. Copland was able to add a soundtrack to the American drama: the expanse of a hopeful nature stuck in the ribs with a stick the size of a heartache. For me, the combination of joy and sorrow can produce a sound that is recognizable: a loneliness that is placed in the crowd, happiness to be lived in the truth of a certain death. I can bring myself to a boil of tears when I think that someday I will die, and I will have to say good-bye to my children; but in such a death I hope there is still faith that makes dying a combination of both sorrow and great joy.

My father likes house plans too. All of my life he has displayed his drawings of his dream house, which he planned to build on some property he bought in Canada in the late 1950s. He will never build that house—he is eighty-seven. But ask him, and he will rebuild each window and door and beam for you right there on the large living room table as he spreads out the huge roll of graph paper with his thin pencil lines. Perhaps you might someday be involved in something like Habitat for Humanity. It seems that you like to build things: organizations, houses, relationships, the health of people.

You wrote of your love for the Colorado mountains. I was in Denver a few months ago for a talk. I arrived at night, gave my talk, and only saw the mountains in the distance as I took the the taxi from the hotel back to the airport. Roe is also drawn to the lure of the mountains. We live in a small town called Pompton Plains in a slight valley. To the west there are worn hills but high enough to cover much of the horizon and pronounced enough to give Roe and me a slight thrill of recognition that there lies something significant. (One Halloween, as I walked with the children, there was a fire on this one hill. It illuminated the sky with its drama. The juxtaposition of the flames and Halloween and the children in their pirate and witch costumes contributed to the mystery of that evening.)

So you have an orderly side too: practical, administrative. I think of people as being like the hand: different parts that make the whole useful. It is clear to me that you have art in your fingers, God in your fingers, order and song and architecture in your fingers. Wouldn't your life be much easier if you collected stamps and worked for the phone company? That you like to organize people and events might tell you something more about your future. We are born with patterns inside of us. We just have to learn how to see the lines and arrows.

You wrote something so very fine and simply true: "It is a fine line for me to walk: to passionately live out all the things that I see as being vital on the one hand, and yet to be content and not always wanting more on the other. How do you push and strive toward the future but not miss the present? I think I struggle with that a lot." If we have an imagination, we risk stability in our ordinary lives for we can, at will, imagine what our lives could be. The more an artist manipulates his or her imagination, the richer the clay feels in the hands but the more that unformed substance becomes the moon or mermaids singing to one another or flowers in a Boston hotel room. And all along, the dog is scratching to be let out or the children are laughing in the yard as they bounce a ball between them. You have hit upon the act of struggle in that statement. What does a young person do with the unanswered questions? Much of what you will have to do is simply to find out for yourself what it feels like to live in the world of passion along with the world of the next car repair bill. I have been blessed with Roe, who keeps me grounded. It has not been easy for her at times. I struggle overtly with my writing self and with my raking-the-lawn self; and sometimes the collision within me spills out, and I make unrealistic requests of Roe. Fortunately she has a sense of humor and faith, and she loves me.

I agree with you, and I have come to the same conclusion but much later in my life: relationships are the most important things, and yet, as you say, complicated. Our relationship with God, our relationship with a wife or husband or lover or children or parents or friends—all are complicated and layered with hidden tricks of passion and truths that need to be sorted out slowly and with faith. I found that true friendship involves great risk…the risk of being rejected. And how far do we invest in relationships? How much do we give? How wide do we open ourselves? How much do we give away? How much do we have to hold back in order to protect ourselves? So much of what you have said about Peter suggests a permanence in the relationship: his ability to listen, his ability to nurture, his ability to speak about the upside-down kingdom, his making you feel completely like yourself. But you said what is perhaps the answer for you now: "I absolutely cannot make the decision of who I am going to be with for the rest of my life without a definitive 'this is the one' from God." There will never be one hundred percent certitude; but there will be a feeling, a surrender to the vocation of marriage coupled with the understanding that marriage is a compromise of sorts. It means pushing aside others (hundreds of others who may fulfill you equally well). But what of God's whisper, "Yes, Liz, this is the man for you"? We can create inside of our minds a vision of paradise or an idea of a spouse that has nothing to do with car repair bills and children laughing in the backyard. We take risks and hook our dreams on a clothesline.

Thank you for sharing so much about your relationship with Peter. In a letter to his son on April 5, 1747, Philip Stanhope, Earl of Chesterfield, wrote "There is a Spanish proverb, which says very justly, *Tell me whom you live with, and I will tell you who you are.*"

I am pleased with the expansive responses to my questions. They reveal your inner nature one word at a time.

I am anxiously waiting for your next letter, to hear about your relationship with God. What does a young woman in Illinois think about such a reality? I have felt all my life that God is like a nagging mother, urging me on to do what is right. I also have felt that God is like Atticus in *To Kill a Mockingbird*...a presence in my life, full of wisdom and love but at a distance, letting me play out my life as best I can without getting in too much trouble. I often think that God is a burden. (It was drummed into me when I was a child that Christopher means "Christ-bearer.") It is difficult to live up to the musical cadence of the Beatitudes —especially "Blessed are the pure in heart."

I have struggled with the heart of a child since I was a child, and it still maintains its fire inside of me. I wrote a novel (as yet unpublished) about the pain of living as an adult with the heart of a child. I remember what it was like to be engaged in the building of a tree fort in the woods with my brother, and that memory of a Saturday afternoon rests just below the surface of my serious, administrative, adult-like self. Perhaps we all have a sense of heaven inside of us, given to us by God at birth, a small relic that will always remind us that the promise of eternity, the promise that that Saturday-afternoon feeling does exist and will be returned to us someday. Perhaps that is God? I think God teaches me with the use of metaphors: What did the tumor in my daughter's foot mean? What was my grandmother trying to tell me the last time I heard her voice over the telephone before she died two weeks later in a Belgian hospital? What is my wife showing me as I give her a long back rub at night as she slowly drifts off to sleep? What does it mean when a friend says "I love you," or when my son beats me at ping-pong? God has taught us through the words of the Bible, but there is so much more too, so many more parables revealed to us each day.

God has taught me through music. I am sure that I would have been a different person if I hadn't stumbled upon Aaron Copland's "Appalachian Spring." When I watched our three children being born, when I press a spoonful of chocolate ice cream to the roof of my mouth with my tongue, when I lift a rock in the yard and see a worm curling away from the light, all are lessons. God teaches us each day. We just have to retain the vision of a child to learn.

I feel in line with myself this evening, as the two planets are in line with each other these past months. Is it Venus and Saturn? I could look it up or ask someone, but sometimes I like knowing part of a story or bits of information. Sometimes it is more fun to believe something based on facts mixed in with a bit of fancy or, usually in my case, something I made up in my own mind. We often live with fabrications, self-deceptions, slight variations of reality to make up for a lost sense for pretending. I pretend I am in the right place in the universe, in the right frame of mind, contained in a sense of accomplishment and gratitude. Much of this is true, but I am also filled with doubts and selfishness and loss, so I look at the two planets lined up in the sky by chance and realize so much of our lives is built on chance orbits circling around a center we cannot identify.

You ask wonderful, hard questions. Do I feel as if I pursue God or is it the other way around? God pursues me.

Do I think that scholarship and faith have a natural communion with each other, or does one water down the other? One drowns the other. To me, much of scholarship can be an individual's pursuit of knowledge in a quest to feel superior to everyone else. People read books, develop theories, extrapolate a self that is wrapped in jargon, and conclude that they have the truth. It is probably a difficult thing to be a theologian in the face of Jesus' saying, simply, "Love one another." I just read a review copy of a new book about the Sabbath. The book is about 200 pages long, all to say, "Keep the Sabbath holy. Rest."

The strong points of being a Catholic? The tradition, the history, the substance of the homilies—and yet these are the strong points of any religion that places God at the center. I often say that there are rules made by humans and rules made by God, and much of the Catholic Church is driven by human-made rules.

But the Catholic Church does a good job, I think, of expressing the God-made rules; but so do the Jewish faith and the Buddhist monks and the Baptists and the Lutherans and the Methodists and the Orthodox Churches. I am all for the unification of churches, and so is this pope. But his idea of unification is according to his rules, not God's rule: "Love one another." Build a universal church on those words.

You asked about the type of books that I read. No, I don't read primarily fiction. I often speak about the novels that have influenced me greatly: *To Kill a Mockingbird*, *Dr. Zhivago*, *Zorba the Greek*, *The Great Gatsby*, and *The Grapes of Wrath*. These are the books that I read between the ages of sixteen and twenty-six. I read *The Brothers Karamazov* in 1990 and was deeply moved. I read very little contemporary fiction, and when I do I am disappointed. I have on my bookshelf the few books of fiction that have added to who I am. Including the ones I've already mentioned, there are Frank O'Connor's short stories, *Treasure Island*, Saroyan's *My Name Is Aram*. I adore Hemingway's Nick

Adams stories, *Alice in Wonderland*, many of Eudora Welty's stories. Perhaps it seems that I read a great deal of fiction, but as a high school English teacher for twenty-two years, I have read a great deal of fiction. (I attribute my being an English teacher to my becoming a writer, for I had to read and read and read when I became a teacher.)

I mostly read nonfiction and poetry. I like biographies of the poets I admire. It would be impossible to list all the poets who have influenced me greatly, but at the top of the list would be William Carlos Williams, Archibald MacLeish, Dylan Thomas, Frost, Pound, Eliot, Wendell Berry, Mary Oliver, Stevens, Yeats. Yes, I am listing the big names, but these people did have a dramatic influence on my writing. I wrote poetry for ten years before I wrote any prose at all. I learned from poetry the power of breaking up the narrative line and the use of music, cadence, pauses, and jumps. Writing poetry has added to what I attempt to do in all my writing: maintain the integrity of what I want to say with the fish-smooth-slippery line of words connected together that will sound, somehow, lovely. The anthropologist Loren Eiseley writes the way I want to write.

My sister-in-law, Lori, gave Roe and me a candle for Christmas last year. It is beige with bits of dark wax floating throughout. Roe has been burning it for two days now that the Christmas season is upon us again. I have been watching the center increase as the small pool of liquid wax grows and grows with each new illumination. Whenever the wick is lit, the wax in the pool becomes liquid. Where there is heat in the center there is a reaction in the outlying areas. We open and close our centers. Sometimes there are hot, liquid events that surround us when we are filled with our own light and heat; but when we are tired or sad or closed, the wax of our lives becomes stiff and holds in place.

I am reading the collected poems of Anne Sexton. I bought each of her new books as they were published. Now her poems have been collected in a hardcover edition, and I could not resist asking for this book as a birthday gift. It has a poignant introduction written by Maxine Kumin. Just reading Ms. Kumin's words and her perceptions about Ms. Sexton's work makes me want to know her.

I understand your desire to read explicit things, rather than fiction. I am often put off by much that is written in fiction for it takes so long to weed through the verbiage to find the magnificent. I find more jarring sensations from reading a poem or an essay—except for books like *To Kill a Mockingbird*, where the music of the writing is sustained from page to page. I like lyrical writing. This reveals much about my own character.

How do children learn, you ask? I believe children learn by watching what adults do, listening to what adults say, and reading what adults read. Parents smoke, kids smoke. Parents read, children read. Parents hit, children hit. Parents love, children love. I have a very simplistic way about how I go about living, Liz. I have been accused of seeing things too much in simplistic terms. Jessie Jackson has a wonderful line: "You do best what you do most." I tell my students that if they smoke a great deal of cigarettes, they will be terrific cigarette smokers. If they watch lots of television, they will become fine television watchers. If they read a great deal, they will become wonderful readers. Now, when it comes to college and employment, people are not looking for great cigarette smokers and television watchers. I am a great advocate of Piaget: Add new knowledge to what we already know, and the combination of the old and new knowledge creates intellectual growth. The old knowledge is changed, and the new knowledge is also altered in the combination. I could say more, but what he said, what he has added to the discussion on how children learn has significantly added to the international dialogue on what we ought to be doing in schools. (That is one reason I believe reading is the key to success.)

You asked about Roe. She and I have been, since the very beginning, independent. She is who she is and I am who I am, and there are many times during the days where we cross purposes and then where we take great delight in each other. It is not my place to challenge Roe in being concerned with the "upside-down kingdom." She has maintained her integrity of self in the face of a demanding husband and in the face of demanding children and in the face of a demanding work schedule. Roe is a giver. She is pulled from many sides of her life and, in the struggle, she has maintained her essential self. We ought not sacrifice who we are by tending to the needs of those we love. We ought to, it seems to me, embrace those we love with who we are. Roe lives the struggles and powers and glories and frustrations of being a woman. She likes to be alone sometimes. She likes to be with me sometimes. She reads, takes long walks, has an honest relationship with God. She knows how to be passionate. She lives with a generous heart, looks at the small picture of each day without worrying about the big picture of an entire life.

What do I do for fun? I have been accused of being a boring person. As a boy I loved ice skating in the winter and swimming in the summer. Today I enjoy driving my 1929 Model A Ford, flying kites with Michael, listening to Karen tell me about her day, visiting a museum, or going on any day trip with Roe. I like looking back in photo albums. I do not have hobbies. I like to read. To answer your question honestly, "What do I do for *real* fun?" Write.

I do have some regrets from my past, and they mostly revolve around relationships. I knew little about extending myself to others as a young adult. I was brought up in a type of social isolation. (It wasn't a bad thing; it was glorious.) My parents moved to this country in 1948 from Belgium with their ideas and language and worlds so different from America. I was born three years later and grew up on two acres with my three brothers and two sisters. I had little contact with other children outside of school. (For me, school was a chore. I attended a Catholic school out of town, so I knew no one except my brothers and sister.)

And yes, I have questioned my own fate at various times in my life, and I do believe that God makes the best out of what we do. I do feel caught in the grip of God's will. I have always felt this. It is suffocating sometimes. To maintain a purity of heart is hard work. I didn't know that when I was your age. My mother said something once that has helped me. She spoke about the church and how the church tries to represent the ideal life that God expects from us. And I have learned that we are human beings, not God. We try and reach the ideal state looking at Jesus as a model. We do have free will; we are human; we have feelings and desires that are gifts and burdens. I realize that we cannot be Jesus, but we just do the best we can. If we honestly try to do the best we can with who we are, we move forward toward the vision Jesus gave us. I do have conflicts with what the world expects of us and with what I believe could be a reality. In many ways, if you want to know what I mean, read *Dr. Zhivago*.

The most important truths I have learned for myself concerning my growing relationship with God? Walt Whitman wrote that perhaps we are all one soul, all people together make for the single ideal. I also feel that God does answer our prayers; that what we seek individually will come to us on this earth, in our lifetime; that certain people come into my life just at the right time, as gifts from God, like ambassadors bearing the good news. Some things like that.

Truths concerning my growing relationship with Roe? She is a divine gift. No one person can fill in the cracks of our brokenness, my loneliness. We need fellow pilgrims for the journey. We need the physical caress of someone who loves us: It is much more fun to go to the ocean with Roe than it is to go there alone. Some things like that.

Truths concerning my growing relationship with my children? I want my children to love each other. They are divine gifts. I have to let them be who they are. I like seeing their fingerprints on the walls. I want to be a father like Atticus. Some things like that.

Truths concerning my growing relationship with my friends? They are divine gifts. Intimacy is essential. They help fill in the cracks of my loneliness.

You asked why I think that you use the word *compelled* a great deal. I even noticed that before you asked the question, and it is a great question. And I believe I know why you use this word. You feel "compelled" by a small voice inside of you to do certain things, so you do it. You have a certain feeling that compels you to write a letter, and I believe that small voice is God whispering. I also believe everyone has that voice deep inside of himself or herself. Some people just listen harder than others. Is this the reason you use that word?

I am glad that you feel compelled to write more because of our correspondence. I also like how open you are with your feelings: thanking me for sharing myself with you in these letters and saying how much you appreciate receiving them. Do you have an inclination of how pleased I am at receiving *your* letters? And do you know that it has taken me ten single-spaced pages to respond to your letter and questions? Yes, words are important. They have the ability to carry the soul of a person, the risk-taking, God-given, life-giving soul of a person.

There is an exhaustion to being a writer that is not unique. Sometimes artists feel a certain patina of grief or obliged suffering that they are due which, they believe, allows them certain privileges: slothfulness among the prime victories. I have read many biographies of writers and find a lot of them to be full of self and complaints against the world. It is easy to be self-absorbed as a writer; for self is the place where it begins, the inner journey, the peeling away, the mining for gold. When self is more mirror than community, there is slothfulness.

I am reading a biography of Rilke. It speaks about the poet's struggle with the barrenness he felt in the face of the world's richness. Rilke felt caught between living in the extremes of life and living in his world of ordinary events.

At one point he seems willing to stop writing altogether as a way to avoid the poison of beauty and the pain that the creation of beauty brings.

This evening as I continued to read the book on Rilke, I noticed that I am having a problem seeing the words. My son asked me what time it was, and when I looked up from my chair and looked at the clock on the wall, I realized that I could not make out the numbers immediately. I strained my eyes a bit and was finally able to tell him it was 8:30. My mother and father, all my five siblings, and two of my children wear glasses. I would like to look like Yeats.

Roe and Karen spent the morning at the physical therapist. (Karen is recovering from knee surgery.) I took Mittens the cat to the veterinarian for her annual shots. Mittens is seven years old. My children were hoping for a cat, an orange cat. I do not know why they wanted an orange cat. I was teaching in a rural high school in northwest New Jersey that year. I asked the students in one of my classes if anyone knew of someone who had kittens to give away. *Every* hand went up. I was in a farm community. "Does anyone have any orange kittens?" Most hands went down, so I spent the that afternoon driving to four different farms. I chose Mittens because she was full of energy and wasn't afraid of me.

I planned to take the Model A Ford out this morning. David drove to work in one car. Roe and Karen took the other car. I wanted to buy *The New York Times* this Saturday morning. It is warm enough today to drive the "A." It is a Ford Tudor built in 1929. I am no mechanic. I just like the physical look of an antique car as I am attracted to the design of an old telephone or an antique ice chest. Some things were beautifully designed fifty and one hundred years ago in such a way that they have retained a quality, a brass-and-wood-and-glass something that is America. I like the wide, round steering wheel of my Ford. I like walking into the garage and smelling the old cushions and wood. Many antique cars have that certain smell. I bought the car from a friend, a retired banker. The headlights look like the bulging eyes of a chrome insect. The body shape is square, boxy, built for the Great Gatsby or the Hardy boys. It is a car Huckleberry Finn and Tom Sawyer would have liked.

As a school administrator I meet many students during the day for various reasons: They need help with a teacher problem; they want a recommendation; they stop in my office to say hello; they would like to know if a course is being offered next year. This afternoon a girl knocked on my open door. My door is always open. "Mr. de Vinck?" she asked. Without even having time to stand up from my chair, the girl stepped in and began to cry a bit. "I failed the state test." Ah, the state test. If a student doesn't pass the state test, the student will not receive a state diploma. I wonder if anyone in Brazil cares if this child doesn't receive a state diploma. I wonder if anyone cares that this student can sing and smile and celebrate and think and fall in love and raise a family and watch her mother die and swim in the ocean and peel carrots and ride a horse and sneeze and eat snow and wear green hats and blow bubbles and dream and weep. But who cares? Those things are not on the state test.

I suppose I should stop writing. Perhaps we can share things in an incremental fashion, letting our lives open up slowly bit by bit instead of trying to jam everything in all at once. (I tend to jam everything in at once in my life.) Perhaps we can exchange letters, writing about the day and events in our lives, but then ask, in the end, one significant question that can propel the other to speak about the upside-down kingdom attached to the ordinary routines of our lives. For example, I am, as I wrote earlier, anxious to hear about your relationship with God. What is your first memory as a child concerning God's presence in your life? Then write about your grammar school days and your high school days, finding, along the way, bits of God's influence in your life. Do you struggle with your faith? What do you hope to attain? Do you feel inhibited because of God's compelled to write to you

watching eye? Hold nothing back in your response. Who is God in your life? Perhaps your next letter to me could be "the religion letter."

Enclosed is a Christmas gift for you. I'd like you to open it on Christmas Day. Perhaps you place gifts under the Christmas tree. It is obviously not an elephant or a hair dryer.

Christopher

Letter Seven

a christmas card

Christopher:

I hope that this reaches you in time for Christmas. I apologize for not writing you sooner after your beautiful *novel* of a letter. Honestly, receiving that letter and generous present sustained me with encouragement and gratitude in the middle of a hellish month of finals, papers, concerts, company visiting, and preparing to be away from Chicago for a month. (Christmas break goes until January 11.)

I was so stressed out that particular day that I cried as I told Peter over the phone what you had sent me. So, in many ways, my simple Christmas greeting does not begin to thank you or address the intriguing topics that surfaced in your letter, but I had to write you all the same and say *thank you* for everything.

This newfound friendship is genuine and comfortable and such a blessing. Thank you for lavishing words and energy onto this stranger from Chicago who loved your book. I promise you will receive a more worthy reply shortly.

Enjoy the season with Roe and your family.

God bless,
Liz

Letter Eight

christmas greetings

Dear Liz:

Your thoughtful card arrived on Christmas Eve. I am pleased that my letter helped in a small way to see you through the difficult few weeks before the Christmas holiday. My son is a freshman at Rutgers, and he felt similar pressures: preparing for exams, anticipating the vacation, the requirement to empty out his dorm suite.

Your simple Christmas greeting, as you called it, was not as simple as you think. Remember, you have extended yourself in friendship all the way from Rochester, Minnesota, to Pompton Plains, New Jersey! Seems to me that this is one of the best Christmas gifts I could receive. (Remember in the card you sent it is written, "Thanks be to God for his indescribable gift!") I include a true friendship in that notion of what is indescribable.

I was sorry to hear how much stress you endured, and I suspect this is just the beginning as graduation and your impending future, fraught with unanswered questions, quickly sets upon you.

Perhaps you do quickly understand that this is a new-found friendship. I am grateful that you sense it is genuine and comfortable and a blessing. There are many things in this troubled world that are false and ugly. When I find what is true and good, I hang on tightly.

I would like you to think about why I lavish words and energy onto a stranger, you, from Chicago. Your parents know why, and your close friends know why. You will develop an even clearer sense of who you are through reflection and experience.

Christmas here was full of peace. Our children were grateful for their gifts. Roe was at peace. (Our children are teenagers now. We actually were able to sleep until 8:00 on Christmas morning!) We spent the morning here and the afternoon at my parents' house. I have spent forty-seven Christmas afternoons at my parents' home. All my brothers and sisters and their children were there. We took a huge family picture at the far end of the living room.

I do not want to write much here for I do not want to interfere with your response to my last letter, which I anticipate with joy. But I did want to say hello and Happy New Year. (I am glad that my new year will include you.)

Christopher

Letter Nine

The Quest

This discussion of a quest sums up some of my greatest struggles and joys in being a Christian and of trying to "keep trying"—to decide to keep letting this part of my life matter so much. As terrible as this sounds, there are days when I have to decide to let it matter, to let faith and my questions and my feelings about this God I can't see or feel or touch or smell control my life, because there are times when I stupidly feel that I could handle things without God.

Dear Christopher:

Greetings from frozen-over Minnesota! It is quite cold here and snowy, a welcome color change at least from the brown, soggy Chicago I left in December. Although now my "other home" is also covered in snow and ice, as even Chicago's O'Hare airport is closed down! I am always impressed with the power of nature. It is presently forty degrees below zero here, with the wind-chill effect at something inhuman like minus seventy degrees. Of course, I was inside all day today, wrapped in my fleece blanket. How abnormal and wonderful it was!

This month off is a wonderful regrouping time. Each year in college I have found this break to be a spiritual, contemplative time, a renewing of my mind and body. (Like most Americans, I am too busy running from task to task; so having an entire month off is a grace-filled respite for me.) It is so nice to have a long stretch of time where I have nothing (at least very little) planned, and things and people come into that time and fill it nicely on their own.

Before I forget, am I not being formal enough if I don't write your address at the beginning of every letter? Inform me on the proper etiquette, if you will, for letters such as these. I have written business letters, which require formal formats, and friend-letters to people I have known forever, but I do not know how to handle these letters to you. From my perspective, you seem too distant if I write your address at the top. I am not saying anything about your making me feel formal by having my address on the letter; I am just wondering.

Today I wrote my bi-annual "personal update letter" for UO (the volunteer organization on campus). I quickly learned to turn this "assignment" to ask people for money into a friendly correspondence where I could keep in touch with people who are important to me. I also use this letter to spread my passion for service and to keep others connected to what I am working on. I will send you one enclosed in this letter or soon to follow. You can see another part of my life that way. The update letter that I wrote today is more personal than previous ones, as it is the last letter of this sort that I will write since I graduate this May.

In writing my update letter, it was personally rewarding for me to look back over my year and to share the highlights with people that I care about, also realizing how extraordinary my last four years have been. People make up a large part of what is important to me wherever I go. I was looking through my old photo albums from when I was twelve years old, and fifteen, and nineteen, and last year's. Always, the people made (and still make) up the most important part of the trip or the class or the dance or the retreat. The events themselves are valuable to a point; but the people account for why I cared about any of it in the first place. I can name off the top ten or fifteen people who have made an indelible difference in my life; most of them are still close friends, and most of them I visited over this break. I wrote a poem once about how each of these persons changed who I am today. When I am with these persons, I try to tell them something of what they have meant to me and to my life; I figure that is the best way to thank them, outside of remaining their friend. I can see how in so many of your books you write about people—family members, children, girlfriends, neighbors, some that you knew well and some that you didn't—all people who left an imprint on your heart.

I have been in a reminiscent mood these past few weeks, with the photo album journeys and being back in my old room, next to my brother's room, hanging out with my parents and high school friends—some people I have known

since I was five, six years old! So that may explain some of
the tones in my voice projected in this letter. My voice, I
assume, will come across differently than my Chicago "I-am-
independent-and-an-adult" voice!

Again, let me thank you for your voluminous writing and
your obvious care about my life. It is still surprising to me
that you keep writing and have such insightful, kind things to
say to me! I greatly enjoy the correspondence and am happy
to hear that you too look extra carefully in the mailbox,
expecting a letter. I hope that this one shan't let you down!
(Is *shan't* a word? It was always in my books by Louisa May
Alcott and L.M. Montgomery, and I have always wanted to
use it; but where the heck does it fit into the English language? ☺) Thank you also for the book you sent. Truthfully,
I haven't cracked it open farther than the table of contents, as
I brought home five books to read and received three others
for presents! So it is on a waiting list, you might say.

To answer some things you asked about in your last letter,
first off, the name *Elizabeth*. I was trying to remember from
your book if you mentioned that name, but I don't think that
you did. What significance does the name hold for you? Yes, I
have thought of what names I would like to name my children: Stephanie, Courtney, Whitney, Taylor, Caleb, Brian,
Zachariah, Bailey, Rebecca—those are ones that I like a lot.
For girls I like romantic sounding names but also with
tomboyish nicknames; and for boys I like creative or solid-
sounding ones.

What do young women my age think about? ☺ Depends
greatly on the woman. I am a female who, for the most part,
denounces her own gender! (Not really, I love women
dearly!) I rarely hang out with a group of girls. I have close
individual female friends and close individual male friends,
but when I am in a group I almost always tend to gravitate
toward the testosterone in the room. In other words, I am not
thinking a lot about what color I look best in, which recipes
to find, what makeup is on sale, or how to be a mom. I don't
mean to sound too strongly anti-woman, I'm really not. I

have my feminine characteristics, like my love for house plans. I have lots of ideas for how to make a home and some of that is through decorating. I like stores like Crate and Barrel and Pier One Imports. I love sappy music and sappy movies, and I do like dressing up when it is called for. Growing up, I saw many dependent girls who would purposely, for example, get lower test grades than their male friends because they didn't want to make the guys feel bad! Or they were without an identity if they did not have a boyfriend. Or they were not allowed to be strong or athletic or smart or aggressive or whatever *simply because they were girls*.

In one way, I want to have boys when I am a parent so that I can teach them to be gentle and loving and sensitive and funny and strong and athletic and to have all the characteristics that both men and women need to have. In another way, I want to have a bunch of girls so that I can teach them to follow whatever dreams they have and not to be afraid of being judged harshly as women. That is a tricky balance. Some people may perceive me as nonfeminine or as a feminist. In pure form I am neither. But I will not keep quiet when I see people, both men and women, hurt by unfair stereotypes put on them by others. If he wants to be a clothing designer, he should be. If she wants to be a doctor, she should be. This has nothing to do with what you asked me! Well, it tells you a great deal about issues that I, at my age, do think about.

College, in a small Christian community no less, is a pretty tricky place to be a "strong" woman. There are spoken and unspoken rules about where girls belong, and I still don't like it. Ironically, I think that I am strongest when I am quiet and gentle and loving, not at the times when I am up-front and leading and sure of myself. But most people don't understand that, so I will let them think that this is how I really am. In a weird way, other girls seem to look up to me when I am in a leadership position, so my strong behavior helps them perhaps. I think that when young women see other women involved and with a strong personality, they can see that they too can exercise such strength.

I also think that the women who are more "feminine" than I am are wonderful people. Many friends of mine want nothing more than to get married and have kids the next year and spend their lives at home or volunteering with their kids, cooking, being their kids' camp counselor, that sort of thing. And what more important job is there than to raise another human being so that he or she feels unconditionally loved and supported? I know that mothering is vital. My mother stayed at home with my brother and me, and it made all the difference. And I may end up doing the same. At this point in my life, I just feel like there are so many other things inside of me; and I don't want someone who doesn't know me or care about me to tell me that I shouldn't or cannot do something simply because of my gender.

Yes, there are things that women tend to be better or worse at when compared to men, but these differences make us all much richer and deeper, not more limited! I think there is a spectrum, and many women tend to be on one end, while many men tend to be on the other end. But there are women and men who completely switch sides! So we all need to be careful to accept one another wherever we may fall on that spectrum.

My mother always told me that I was the most strong-willed child she knew. My favorite phrases as a two-year-old were "I do. I do," and "Up. Up." I always wanted to do things on my own and to be thrown up into the air, and I repeated my requests all the time! Maybe those are the things in our personalities from the time we are zygotes. Maybe I learned it from being a smart girl who wasn't willing to get bad grades to win attention from boys. Maybe it was because I had friends who were anorexic, whose parents told them boys would never look at overweight girls. Being strong-willed is a big part of who I am though. People who know me best like that trait in me and even bring it out, like Peter. He is more of a feminist than I am! And my brother, one of my closest friends, is at sixteen years old already a compassionate, friendly, strong, gentle-hearted guy who both men and women love to be with. These are the kind of people that this world needs.

Also, a side note: I love the humor of guys and the way that they will usually tell you what they are thinking about and are much more honest and frank than well-meaning women. I deal better with that than with small talk or beating around the bush. Blather wears me out faster than an emotional confrontation does! This is a long answer to your question, but this is one issue that I think about because I am in the process of defining myself.

You have said several times that you cannot believe that I think the way that I do at my age. Tell me why that is. In a way I understand what you are saying but for the most part I don't. You said something in an earlier letter about how you "started young" in thinking about the scales of the upside-down kingdom and such. Did you have some particular epiphany that led you to drastically change your thoughts? I know that there are some specific things that have contributed to how I think and maybe my memory is too subjective, but I think that I have always pretty much thought this way. I mean, if I had written you at fifteen I would have discussed many of the same things. Hopefully my grammar and vocabulary, and possibly humor, are better now or at least more refined. But the content would be largely the same.

There are times when I am attracted to the other scale too, when I think that I would be better off grabbing that economically secure job and marrying someone with a great resume of qualities, sure to boost me into the stratosphere of fame, popularity, wealth, and security. But if you are at all a thinking, perceptive, or tiny bit emotional person, you can't look at the way things are in this world and think that these are the true answers or the way to be happy and fulfilled. Maybe it is my perfectionistic side shining through. Why live life halfway? Why give in to what others tell you is best? Why settle for less than making an eternal difference and being everything that you can be? (Maybe I watched too much *Sesame Street* as a kid with those motivational "be all you can be" statements. "Brought to you by the color green and the number 7.") At any rate, I always wonder why it surprises you that I am the age that I am. Maybe simply that we have so much in common? But I would think that there are many people my age with bright eyes and dreams and passion. Finding an older adult in the "real world" who has held onto that vision is more difficult.

I also want to comment on something that you said in the last letter. You said, "Do you know that you have much confidence in who you are?" And then later you commented on how you also experience the reality of being pulled in many directions, sometimes your "writing self" and your "raking-the-lawn self" clash. Also you commented on how people will always be in need of something from us, and the trick is to know when to love and give and when to self-preserve.

I often feel that I am not confident in myself, like I am trying to be everything and I am not really anything. I can see myself being absolutely anything, having almost every characteristic; yet sometimes I feel that all that leaves me as being not very much of anything. I don't mean for that to sound self-deprecating; it's just restlessness, feeling that I am not going to end up being what I desperately want to be or feel that I should be.

How do you reconcile those selves and know who you are? Are we all really a crazy mix-up of almost every trait, and we end up developing different ones because of our circumstances? How do you sound so content with who you are and the decisions that you have made and the way that the future goes? I think that I am often afraid that I will miss "the way," like one of my favorite quotes speaks of. Actually, it is a good segue from this part of my letter to the part that you requested. So, here begins "The Religion Letter":

Here is my quote. Read it once, then a second time to absorb it.

> To *believe actively* that our Heavenly Father *constantly* spreads around us providential circumstances

that work for our present good and our everlasting well-being brings to the soul a veritable *benediction*. Most of us go through life praying a little, planning a little, jockeying for position, hoping but never being quite *certain* of anything, and always secretly afraid that we will miss the way. This is a tragic *waste of truth* and never gives *rest* to the heart.

There is a *better* way. It is to repudiate our own wisdom and take, *instead* the infinite wisdom of God. Our *insistence* upon seeing ahead is natural enough, but is a real hindrance to our spiritual *progress*. God has charged himself with full responsibility for our eternal happiness and stands ready to take over the management of our lives the moment we turn in *faith* to him.

—A. W. Tozer
The Knowledge of the Holy

In many ways this quote encompasses my personal spiritual quest. *Quest* is the appropriate word to be used here, as I see myself as a seeker, one who questions and changes and is not easily satisfied in my pursuits. I italicized the words in the quote that most affect me. I have this one memorized, almost by accident, simply from my rereading it so many times. This discussion of a quest sums up some of my greatest struggles and joys in being a Christian and of trying to "keep trying"—to decide to keep letting this part of my life matter so much. As terrible as this sounds, there are days when I have to decide to let it matter, to let faith and my questions and my feelings about this God I can't see or feel or touch or smell control my life, because there are times when I stupidly feel that I could handle things without God. It never lasts very long, and then I am back in God's embrace and learning again the truths that I learned when I was six and twelve and sixteen! I guess this quote speaks to me ideas of surrender, letting God be God, and the fact that we have a dependable God. All very important. Here are some more specifics:

Believe actively—That's a big one for me. I have often fallen into the pattern of doing what is good simply because everyone else does it. I grew up in a moral, upright, religious town. Most of my friends seemed like good, kind people. It was not difficult to be that way, until I realized how much I detested being fake, to myself or to others. Actively believing means more than saying a statement at church or reasoning out belief for a paper in class. It means that you risk your own life decisions on the precept that you believe, you know, you are intellectually and emotionally certain that God will do what God says. Without active belief I think that religion becomes a topic to discuss (or avoid, I suppose) or another category to slot people into. That is why discussing it makes me so excited: It is active; it changes; it is based on people and what they see of God—which makes a difference in everyone's life.

Constantly—This to me suggests dependability, greatness. God is always looking out for me, always awake to listen, always able, always aware, always interested in my life. That's very important.

Benediction—This is something that a restless, questioning, questing person like myself longs for: to have rest, to have relief in my *heart*, no less! Especially when I was younger, I was certain that knowing all the answers would bring rest to my soul. Then, when I was much wiser (all of fourteen years old), I thought that being pure-hearted and truly loving people all the time would bring me rest. Then, when I was in high school, I considered that neither of those endeavors could be attained and that God must just want me to love everyone. I am still learning new ways to see God's desire for each person now, at the end of college; but I have never really found rest. In some ways I doubt that I ever will, but that's an OK price to pay for being thoughtful and aware and sensitive. At this point in my life, my soul receives some relief when I am reminded that I do not have to know all the answers, that I will never be truly pure in heart or able to love everyone, and that it is not necessarily easy to know God.

Certain—Another word that is linked somewhat to the previous idea. Being a biblical studies major and also being fairly well-read and intelligent growing up, I struggle with knowledge and the pride and barriers that these things can create. I cannot tolerate people who never think or never let intellectual reasoning have any sway in the world of religion. A phrase like "faith isn't faith until it's all you're holding on to" is misleading, in my opinion. Faith is still based on a thought process, not just a warm feeling. Abraham and the disciples were given something and someone to have faith in —and so are we. As a younger Christian I felt terribly guilty for having questions and, heaven forbid, even doubts about God and about the very nature of my religion. I put off such doubts for a long time, but they came out much stronger when I finally faced them straight on and admitted that these intellectual assents were important to my faith.

The God of the Bible gave people things that they could think about, a person to trust who was worthy of faith, a person who was able to be known. So I refuse to never use my mind, although I agree that it is dangerous when you use only your intellect in matters of faith.

Waste of truth—I love this phrase. It seems to say that there is all this truth already out there, free for the taking, if people would just stop planning and praying their want lists and giving in to their own knowledge and their own fears. If we continue that way, we are wasting the truth, wasting the efforts of God who is capable of giving the soul a true benediction, who is constantly spreading things in our lives that are just waiting to be accessed. I like that idea.

Rest—Another word like *benediction*. Giving rest and relaxation, taking weight and responsibility and worry off of me, and placing it instead on the truth.

Better and *Instead*—These words seem to say that this way that God is showing us, this truth is better than the lies that we live off of. We tend to waste truth with busyness, our self-satisfaction, laziness, and worldly standards, even though these things do not compose the best, highest, deepest, or richest life that we could be participating in. And, like I said before, why bother if we are not going to pursue the deepest life that there is to live? The *instead* part means to me that we have to die (at least in part if not completely) to the primary way of planning and praying and jockeying, if we want to access the relief and truth found in trusting God. *Instead* of my way, God's way. *Instead* of the known, comfortable way, *instead* of ease and fame—perhaps the way of the cross.

Insistence—This word makes me think of someone, um, well, let's see…me! ☺ Insistent, compelled, driven, passionate, all those great adjectives that are wonderful and deep and maybe somewhat attractive but also difficult to live with. My insistence can, sometimes, be the very thing that wastes the truth in my life, that makes me unable to find relief and rest.

Progress—If life is a progression (i.e. not a state of being or an answer or a final goal that we just have to arrive at), it makes things more understandable and more livable! I want to progress in whatever scales that I think are best, but I don't believe that God makes it so that we are either right or wrong. So no one has "completely arrived" or is totally doomed; we have chances every day to follow God or not to.

Faith—This is really the driving force of Tozer's entire quotation. If we have faith enough to turn over the management of our lives to God, if we sincerely want to have someone bigger and more capable (not ourselves) running our lives, then we must turn, choose the better way, give up our own will to the One who is able take our lives and do what God wills with it. This is how one finds truth, finds rest, finds God.

I hope that these explanations have made sense. They might be muddled as it has gotten late, and my mind is winding down! But I want to answer more of the questions in your letter, and so tomorrow I will start by addressing those.

Good night.

Now it is Thursday morning, and I have read over my mostly coherent letter to you! You asked about my specific memories of God, of my history of encountering God, so to speak. My earliest recollection of God is when I was probably four or five. I was watching a commercial that had homeless people in it. The announcer was explaining the pictures and trying to evoke a money response from viewers. I remember sitting close to the television and weeping because the woman on the screen looked so sad and so lonely. I knew, even at that early age, that that wasn't right and I knew that I would feel horrible if I was outside in the cold rummaging through a dumpster searching for food. (That may be a small reason that I am still so involved in trying to improve the lives of homeless people through my volunteer activities.)

When I looked at that homeless woman I cried so much that my mother heard me and came in the room to see what was wrong. When I explained to her why I was so upset and how I felt as if I couldn't help the lady on the screen, my mother smiled and said that there was only one person who could really help everyone and that was God. She said that God was able to love and care for and feed everyone but needed human help to accomplish that goal. I have always seen God as a comforter, maybe from experiences like that.

The other specific memory that I was told about and remember somewhat on my own is when I "asked Jesus to come into my heart" at age five. I had asked my parents to teach me how to read soon after the commercial incident, and I learned quickly. Then I read what I could of my children's Bible. I was told that I asked my parents to teach me how to read because I wanted to read the Bible. Then I explained to my mom that I wanted to follow this person Jesus, but I didn't know how. She whispered to me that the first step was to pray and tell Jesus that I believed in him and wanted to follow him and that I needed him in my life. From this point on, my history with God is murky in the sense that I do not see God entering in at specific times or places. But God has always been there.

You asked about my parents. My mother had a hard childhood and experienced some abuse that led to her being raised by her loving and hard-working grandmother. She never had positive experiences with the church and even remembers the pastor visiting her poor grandmother who was raising two kids by herself to ask for money and scolded the family for not attending church. She did not become a Christian until she attended college. This difficult childhood, of course, still affects who my mother is today and why she struggles with what she does. Her more secular background and apprehension toward the church has affected my life too.

My father is a quiet, gentle, loving man who tends to be perfectionistic and very introverted. He grew up in a stoic, Lutheran home and went to college desperately wanting *true* religion, something that was personal and expressive. I think that my father loved his parents a lot, but they never knew how to express that they accepted him, which explains his struggle with a religion that he "inherited" from them. Again, this feeling of needing "genuine religion" that my dad struggled with defines part of who I am today.

Both my parents were in an "underground" Bible study group in college that met against the wishes of school authorities because they discussed ideas not sanctioned by the school. This group talked about questions and fears that they had and dealt with the *reality* of their faith. My parents went on two dates within two weeks after being in this study group for more than a year together; they were engaged that second week of dating! Ever since their marriage, church life was in the forefront of their lives. I was brought up hearing stories from my parents—knowing that trusting people simply because they are supposed to be good to you or because they are in authority is not always valid, that revolutionary thinking changes people and issues, and that being what everyone else wants you to be will not bring happiness. I also always knew that the church can disappoint people. It does not extend its hands and heart as far as it should, and God often has to fix the mistakes of the church. Sometimes that gap between the church and God's intentions for it frustrate me to no end! And yet, I myself am part of that problem too, as I am a sinful human being along with all other churchgoers.

My parents were one of ten couples that branched off from the First Covenant Church in Rochester and formed the church that we attend now, Salem Road Covenant Church. I was the first baby baptized there, went to Sunday school every week, sang in the junior choir that my mother directed, played the piano for offertory, completed my confirmation at fourteen, was very active in the youth group with a core group of friends, participated in Bible camp every summer from ten to eighteen years old, was a "Bible Quizzer" in the Quiz League at church, took school friends to Vacation Bible School in the summer and Christmas Eve service in the winter, counseled at camp when I was old enough, arranged special music regularly, helped in the Chicago mission trip we took, had potlucks with families there every other week. I still consider my best friends to be the people that I grew up with there and basically was enveloped by my church's culture as far back as I can remember.

My parents had a painful break with the church when I was a senior in high school and they left, trying other churches for three years and never feeling whole or resolved or happy. Just this last year they tried going back to their old church, and it was an amazing, emotional day. People have been welcoming and loving ever since. I have learned a lot about forgiveness and hope from that experience.

All of this defines much of who I am with God. I have never doubted God's existence or need for me to be part of God's plan to change this world. I am not, however, what I call a "campy," peppy sort of Christian, someone who answers every problem and question with "God will take care of it." I could have easily been that way, not hearing people's real concerns because of my own ideas about God; but I couldn't be because of the reality that I saw staining all those simple answers. Yes, God is in control of my mother's life, but why was she as an innocent child forever marred by abuse if God is always in control? Why, if God is in control, didn't God make my father's parents more loving and encouraging so that he would feel accepted? Why, if God is in control, are there so many problems in a church, even one filled with kind-hearted people? Why so many disagreements and resentments and anger? Why, if God is in control, do people I idolized at my Bible camp have children at seventeen and get divorced and fall away from their fiery faith? I almost threw out religion a couple of times in my life when I dealt with those issues, but instead I was left with a more realistic, sustainable faith in the refining process, one that is hopefully based more on what God is trying to do in the world and not on the failures or successes of people.

I am confused still, though, on where the lines should be drawn. I talked with my sixteen-year-old brother and his friend who are just starting to really care about this process with their own personal faith, and they have many questions. Why go to church just because their parents want them to? Why are some Christians hypocrites, and why does the church tolerate that? Why do strong Christian people still have problems in their marriages? I wonder, as they do; but I have added more realism to the question, I guess.

From my limited knowledge, I think that Christian marriages can go wrong just as secular ones do, if the people involved don't make a concerted effort to grow daily in love for the other person. I think that pastor's kids or people who grew up attending Bible camp can struggle with drugs and premarital sex and all those worldly issues if they are in the wrong environment or if they do not see good examples. Struggling with these things doesn't mean that we are not Christians, just that we are human and flawed in essence; and we have Christ and the church to help support us through that. That is where the role of Christians in the church can be so vital. We need to live out the ideals and put aside our pettiness. We are all in the process of being changed into the image of Christ.

I still struggle with my faith in this aspect. There are absolutes, and yet I waver on where those lines may fall or if they are the same for everyone. And where does that leave the answers to questions such as the ones my brother and his friend were asking? Are you less of a Christian if your marriage fails? if you struggle with drugs? Why do we pinpoint certain visible issues as ones that make another Christian "weak," such as doing drugs or being promiscuous but not other less obvious sins, like selfishness, spiritual pride, or anger?

There is no one perfect way to be a Christian, but there do seem to be some things that strongly detract from the process. I don't want to limit the holiness and wonder of God. God's just and all-knowing ability to see everyone's heart and mind means that God sees inside the souls of camp counselors and of all of us and our choices. Those things hurt God and pull us away from God. But on the other hand, I also believe that God specializes in mercy. Does that mean that a broken marriage or an addiction or something similar would have to be "overcome" to mean that a person was really "back on his or her feet" spiritually? Or can we ever really judge one another? What if we all sin, all the time, and there really is no way to say, "I have conquered that problem. I am over that temptation"? That could be a good thing, because it keeps us dependent and returning to God. What if the point isn't to ascend to some relationship or understanding but to surrender and settle into a loving, growing admittance that we need God? I sometimes hear threads of this message preached, but more often I hear pastors admonishing us for being too easy on ourselves and telling us how God has set strict standards that we have to follow.

I struggle with how much my outward actions mean compared to my internal state of heart and mind. I have an easy time being nice and friendly and loving outwardly, but I can be selfish, proud, or jealous on the inside and no one would know. I think it is a shame when a church congregation acts as if it has it all together, when in reality it ought to be a place to deal with the honest struggles of life. I once read a quote: "Church is a hospital for sinners, not a showcase for saints." How different most churches would act if they truly believed that. Even as I write of this notion, upside-down in many ways, I question it. Do I really want to say that the broken, drug-addicted, divorced, angry, fallen, weak woman is more along the lines of what God desires for us than the organized, happy, well-adjusted, confident, outgoing, encouraging, peacemaker of a woman who has been successfully married for twenty years? (I realize that the issues aren't as polarized as these two lists depict.)

I hope that this has made some sense to you. I realize that I was writing almost stream-of-consciousness style. I read back over these last few pages to try to summarize or organize my thoughts more, but I couldn't do it! I was basically explaining struggles that I have: with what a Christian should aspire to be—broken or strong and how that relates to my outward actions, standards, and absolutes, and how this all affects churches. You asked what I hope to attain. These last few pages show you some of the problems that I have in discerning what I should be trying to attain. Truthfully, I often want to be the second woman in the list I wrote above: someone who possesses all those traits and more, so that everyone (including me) knows without a doubt that I am in the arms of the Lord and steadily moving upward with my life. But I really don't think that that is the answer. I still have many questions about what the goal should be. For now I know that I need to work on my relationship with God. God has always seemed to me to be close, present, aware of my life, and even interested in it! I rarely feel inhibited, as you asked, by "God's watchful eye." If God is watching, it is to help and comfort. Sometimes I worry that I disappoint God because I feel so unsure of where to head or where God wants me to go, and I know that there is so much going on of eternal significance. I don't want to miss a second of life, I suppose. I don't want to miss what God is doing.

The names that I use for God are usually *Father* and *Lord*, sometimes *Jesus* or *God*. My father, to me, displays much of who God must be. (I read in my psychology textbook that people often see God with the same weaknesses and strengths that they see in their earthly fathers. Imagine all the brokenhearted, confused boys whose fathers were never happy with them or the women who were abused and can't relate to feeling loved.) I see God as being strong through humble, gentle, loving power. I do not see God as being loud or showy or proud. I see God as knowledgeable and dependable and available. (My father and I would sit up late and talk, even when he had to get up for work in three hours. He would listen to me and answer me, and he always tried to understand the best that he could.) I see my heavenly Father as being purposeful, relational, playful, creative, and impressive. I have never understood people who feel that they cannot come to God. God has never scared or intimidated me. I see God as one who, like the father of the prodigal son, waits for his children to come home. I am still learning how this image fits with God as warrior or God as jealous and harsh, for these are biblical aspects of God's character as well.

I see God as having high standards and infinite love and patience for us to arrive. I know that God sees when I try, even when I fail. God's presence in my life is my biggest motivation to be on the scale of the upside-down kingdom. I remember in your reply to my first letter you said that I seemed like someone who wanted to be validated for being on the upside-down scale. I know that God sees it and that is ultimately worth it to me, but I also want the world to understand and embrace that standard as well.

God is the ultimate reason behind what I do, even when I don't know what it is that God wants from me or how I should do it or what to do after I am guilty of failing somehow. God will always take me back and love me just the same. The least I can do is seek God—hence, my quest! ☺

I hope that this has conveyed to you the truth about how I feel about God. I talk about this area a lot and love to think about it, but I have not written down this much and studied it this closely before. It has been good for my faith to examine it and give language to it like this. Also, I will have to tell you more in another letter about the negative parts of my faith. This letter makes me sound too sure, too convinced, and too confident of God and of my faith. That is an unfair picture, as

I am very unsure and frustrated and scared and sick of the whole thing at times. I have a hard time combining spirituality with reality. That is where the problem comes in for me. This letter may have portrayed more my idealistic version of God. I am feeling close to God and idealistic, being here in my home and relaxed on a vacation. I shall tell you about my feelings some dark, wet, dreary evening when I can't get any answers and I feel alone and tired and worn out and feel like nothing in my life amounts to anything, because I want you to know that I definitely experience those nights too, as well as the comforting, uplifting, "I love having these high standards" nights! Feel free to ask me to explain what I have written or to discuss things that you disagree with. I will not be offended or hurt, and we would probably both grow and benefit from the challenge. I again apologize, for this is all muddled; but how does one organize writing about someone as meaningful and pervasive as God? (That's my excuse anyway!)

This letter needs to end—it is already noticeably jammed with information! I hope that you had a wonderful holiday and start of the new year. Again, thank you for the generous present and your continued, genuine friendship and energetic letters. I am refreshed, encouraged, and enlightened by your thoughts and by who you are. Thank you so much for letting me see so much of you and responding to my passion for being deep and questioning. I will not pose another upside-down scale question for you at the end of this letter, for there are already plenty of questions in these pages for you to digest!

Have a wonderful day whenever this letter arrives in your mailbox, and respond to my Chicago address, please. I leave for my "other home" this Sunday to start my last semester of college!

Warmly,
Liz

Letter Ten

The Delights of friendship

I did not plan to have such a correspondence in August. I didn't know you existed in August. Isn't that strange and hopeful? To think that there are people waiting for us, people we have not yet met but who will have a deep influence on who we are?

Dear Liz:

I am writing to you five hours after receiving your letter from Minnesota. I do not know anyone from Minnesota. There is something foreign and wild and perhaps even wonderful about that part of the country: the history of trappers and the vision of all that farmland. I know it is where Sinclair Lewis lived and where Judy Garland was born and where Charles Lindbergh grew up. I also know that Minnesota is the source of the Mississippi River. (I like that, the source of the American bloodstream.)

When I fly to the West Coast for a talk, I look out the window of the aircraft and pretend that I am taking the entire nation into my hands, like a *National Geographic* map spread out before me. Here the green of the New England states, then suddenly a stretch of patchwork farms. There the Mississippi, the spine of America, and there the Rocky Mountains, the desert, the moon in Oklahoma. I like flying at night too, imagining each light belonging to someone: families, grocers, a light hung out by the barn, street lamps perhaps, the miles of homes and territory, people I will never meet, towns I will never visit, possibilities that will never be cradled into my life. There is a sadness about the vastness and the lost relationships that are impossible to discover, develop, maintain. That is one of the many reasons that I like being writer. At least I will meet people part way, they hearing my voice, but my being denied the returned response. I think about my books in that library or in that apartment building. Someone found my little stories, heard a voice from New Jersey. Some people write (☺), some call me on the phone. Most never respond.

Over the Christmas vacation Roe and I traveled to New York City for a visit to the Metropolitan Museum of Art. I like the sculptures the most: the human figures carved from stone, muscle and arms and beauty chipped away from a mass of rock; these things startle me. Here and here and here, and suddenly a woman in stone. That relationship between the artist and the stone consists of a certain power to imagine a form and create the form, though all along the form is not the reality, just a hint, an expression. But there is delight and solace. I feel that when I fly over the country. I imagine myself scooping up a nation, much like Walt Whitman felt, the entire soul of a nation, and making something of it. It is not the nation, of course, but the image, the hint, something sad and beautiful all at once. There are many powers beyond us: the weather, as you say, and the muse, the IRS, the fragility of our bodies held in the power of the spirit.

I cannot imagine what minus forty must be. You tell me it is that cold in Minnesota! I have never been in such cold. I think of curling smoke and lambs' wool on a barbed wire fence and pine trees and snow when I think of minus forty. Can it be that where you live it is so cold? Is it possible?

I am glad that you had this past month of peace. My son had the same amount of time from Rutgers. He returns this Sunday. Roe was a bit annoyed that David didn't work for these four weeks, but I told her that I never worked on my college winter vacations; and I think David could, like you, use the break, the time for reflection, the time to clear his mind a bit. Roe has worked since she was sixteen. In high school and all through college she worked for a supermarket, working there every weekend and every holiday and vacation.

One of the first times I brought Roe home to my house there had been, recently, a wild storm of great wind and rain. The largest tree on the property, perhaps sixty, eighty feet tall, had fallen onto the side lawn. It lay there for a

number of weeks like a dead whale. When Roe saw that, she
wanted to grab a saw and cut the tree up for my father. She
couldn't understand why it was still there, crushing the garden. Roe is a worker. (So you can see why she wants David
to get a vacation job.) When I first met Roe she reminded
me in many ways of Antonia in Willa Cather's novel, *My
Antonia* (the book I mentioned to you earlier). Antonia was
a strong woman of deep goodness who clearly understood
what was essential, who never stopped working and living,
among life's ups and downs, with a will to survive.

When Roe was a sophomore in college, her mother died
of undetected stomach cancer. Her father died a few years
later. She had no relationship with her father. He was a simple man who did the best he knew how, the father of a girl
he would never understand or know. Roe's mother loved her
unconditionally, and that has made all the difference.

The informality of your letters, with your writing ability,
makes your letters sound familiar, alive, filled with unre-
strained charm and a freshness that you are not even aware
of. I think in your question of formality and writing an
address at the beginning of your letters to me shows that
you recognize that our correspondence is not typical or not
what is usual—perhaps not usual in this modern, e-mail,
postcard, nonletter-writing telephone age. And yes, business letters are easy to understand and letters to a friend
you have known for a long time, those are easy to catego-
rize and to figure out how they are to sound or look; but
what of a stranger you had not known except in a few
letters and books? I hope you do not detect a distant formality in my letters to you, but then I also hope you see
that what I have been *compelled* to do is write you in a way,
with a tone of voice, with a certain lean-back-in-my-life way
that is really my writing voice, my more than outside true
self that may at times slip into a literary-like formality that I
do not plan or intend.

You suggested the notion in your letter when you said
much of what you wrote was a stream-of-consciousness

narration on your thoughts about God. That is, I believe, one of the hidden writing tools that can be had after a great deal of reading and writing and living. The fluid quality of prose, when placed in the context of a writer's heart and deep purpose to be heard and understood, is refined with each day, after reading another book, and after trusting God's gift or desire that the writer, well, writes. I am glad that you sense just by placing an address at the top of a page there is the feeling of distance, a wall separating the writer and reader. I like how sensitive you are to such small things. I often write my address at the end of a letter to a friend, making it easier to find the address if he or she wants to write back. There is something romantic too when someone writes me a letter that ends with an address from, oh, Paris or Minnesota, that faraway place, a distant correspondence. I read often the collected letters of writers and enjoy seeing where they were when they wrote to a friend or publisher. The format of our correspondence is formed by the developing nature of two people who, by fate, met, cared, and wrote. One of the things that I promised myself about my life with Roe and the children was to create a home where we can all be who we are, comfortable in who we are, free to be who we are. What will mean the most to me in our letters is that you can be completely comfortable, that you can be yourself, that you can say anything to me, and that these letters will add to your developing nature. You know what happens to a seed that is planted in rich soil. Do not forget too that your letters have given me yet another place in my life where I can grow, where I can be who I am essentially. Minnesota is the source of the Mississippi. We discover the source of ourselves from the people we love.

You spoke about this so well as you looked through your photo album. We are who we are through the cumulative influence of people around us. That is one of the reasons why I am so cautious about praise from people concerning my writing. I am a writer because of all the books that I have read, because of all the editors and agents who believed in my work, because of my mother, and because of God and grace. When people step up to me and say how much they love my work, they are really saying how much they love what I have read and whom I have loved; and they are also saying how much they love themselves. If you were to stack the influences that pressed upon a writer's heart in a single pile you would see the enormous need an artist has for stimulus in order to create a bit of story or poem or sculpture. Praise the artist, and we neglect the community. Praise the work alone, and we neglect God. Something created without grace and God is never art. Never. Your letters are filled with grace and God, and I believe that if you keep grace and God close to your heart during these next months, you will feel compelled to choose the next step in your life. You will feel it, just as you feel that same intuition when you write in a stream-of-consciousness style. The words come if you are genuinely trying to be God's child and genuinely trying to do God's will.

You will have, for all of your life, times when you slip into that reminiscent mood. It is what I wrote earlier to you . . . it is your reflective nature. And it hurts, Liz, sometimes. I know. But it is also, well, like looking down at all of America from an airplane: all that beauty and sadness, all those lives of people we will never meet, and filled with people we have met. The landscape of our past is filled with color and sounds and missed opportunities and victories. My father is eighty-seven years old. What does he see when he looks out that window?

Your thanks to me for writing you pleases me, especially in your honest words, ". . . and obvious care about my life." But you do understand that what you receive from my letters is very much what I receive from yours. You are amazed a bit that I would choose, out of all the people I have met, to write to you with such care and attention? But Liz, don't you see it is the same with me, how amazed I am that of so many letters you receive and so many people you meet, you chose to send me such an extraordinary first letter, and you continue to pour your true self into this correspondence? I am grateful that you have such an interest and trust in me as well. I did not plan to have such a correspondence in August. I didn't know you existed in August. Isn't that strange and hopeful? To think that there are people waiting for us, people we have not yet met but who will have a deep influence on who we are? That it is still surprising that I write to you tells me that you are still delighted and puzzled. I hope the delight lasts a lifetime, that is one of the many joys of friendship; and I hope the puzzlement disappears in time. I like how you think, how you write, how you respond to what compels you, that you recognize the power of the upside-down kingdom. It should be no surprise that people like you. Also, these letters have been very important to me as a writer, for you have give me a chance to write about some things that I have not yet written about, which brings me to something I wanted to say later on in this letter but am reminded just now. I think I made a mistake when I suggested that we stick to one topic per letter or something like that. Please, just go back to writing what you feel, asking questions, speaking about the day or the heart according to what urges you forward. To place any restrictions on our letters or to impose any sort of format will, I believe, hurt in a little way the vigor and freshness of what we write. I truly believe that these letters are a holy place for both of us. I too am excited about your letters. And *shan't* is a great word! And don't ever worry about disappointing me in what you write. A letter written with attention and risk is a gift no matter how long or short. If it is genuine, there is never any disappointment. (What were the other books you brought home to read and the three you received as gifts?)

The name Elizabeth is the name of the only other woman I asked to marry me. I met her when I was a junior in college, and I fell in love with her. I dated many women in high school and college, beautiful women: a ballet dancer, an education major, a French major, the brightest graduate student at Columbia University, a girl with the most beautiful hair, a young woman who wanted to make love to me within an hour of our meeting. Liz, I was a terribly lonely young man. Human beings have sexual passions that need to be expressed. God gave us this passion. I wanted to make love to a woman I was in love with, so after dating a woman for a while and realizing that I was not falling in love with the person, I ended the relationship. It was so difficult for me to do. Well, then I met Elizabeth. Everyone called her Betty. I fell in love with her. She was majoring in art, was a silversmith who made beautiful silver jewelry, especially bracelets and necklaces. She worked with children with mental handicaps in the summer, collected children's books, loved the theater, made me laugh. We had a relationship for two years, but we hardly kissed...held hands a great deal, spent many hours together, attended classes together, went to Broadway plays and restaurants. I was going to wait for her to come around. What I didn't realize was that she wasn't falling in love with *me*. I remember the first time I began to realize this. We were at her home and she wanted to show me this beautiful sports jacket she sewed herself. She created the pattern, bought the material, cut the lining. It was a beautiful man's sport jacket, which she made for one of her male friends, not for me. She would hardly let me touch her; she always wanted me to come over, to take her here and there. I think, probably now that I look back, she liked someone being in love with her, liked the attention, and was trying to figure out if it would all lead to love; which it didn't. When I asked her to marry me (we were driving down an off-ramp to a highway—how about that for romance?), she sat there for a moment, turned and told me that, no, I was too good for her. I never knew what she meant by that, but I will tell you this: I knew then, and I know now what it means to love someone. It is not a frivolous, superficial thing, for me at least, when I say that I love someone in the way that is lasting and forever. If you love a person in that way it doesn't go away. In many ways, for me, having lost Betty in my life has been equivalent to having lost someone to death … the pain never goes away. It is not debilitating, but it is always there. I loved Betty with all that I knew as a young man. I never saw her again. We ended the relationship for good in January 1974. I know the month and the year because it was in that month and year that I began my writing career.

I was so painfully alone and depressed and sad. I was in the graduate dorm. I had choices; I was in desperate need of soothing my sadness. It seemed to me that most people around me were making love, drinking, and/or smoking, inhaling, or ingesting one drug or another. These were all available freely and easily at Columbia in 1974. I didn't want to make love to a woman I wasn't in love with. I didn't want to drink or get involved with drugs. I didn't know about the power of prayer and was not an overtly faithful person. I loved Betty, and how do you replace what was lost? I began to write poetry. Betty became the muse, and I tried to recreate her in the beauty of words. From the greatest loss in my life I was horribly shaken into becoming a writer. I think this is the epiphany you asked about. It was at this time that I discovered the poetry of William Carlos Williams, and then I read probably every poem of his that was ever published in America.

Betty became less and less the muse. She was and still is a part of who I am, but the center of my writing is now also filled with Roe and the children and regret about Betty and the joy of Michael saying to me last week, "Dad, I had a dream last night. You and I were driving in the car and we saw this beautiful bald eagle with a red tail." The muse is Roe suggesting that we go out and cut that tree apart in my father's garden and Willa Cather and Gatsby and Dr. Zhivago and the music of Aaron Copland and the nation spread out before me on my *National Geographic* map that sits on my lap under a pen. The muse for me is now the dancers of Degas and my daughter whispering in the darkness as I draw down her shade, "I love you, Daddy." The muse is Roe calling me on the phone at work to remind me to take Michael to fencing lessons.

Had Betty married me there would have been no Roe, Karen, David, Michael. I would not have become a writer. I probably would not have met you. The sequence of our lives can be looked upon as chance or design. I choose design. These are the reasons why the name *Elizabeth* is so wrapped up in who I am. Karen's middle name is Elizabeth. Elizabeth is a significant name.

What do young women think about? I like your smile after that statement, but I didn't know what the smile meant. I was pleased to hear your attitudes about being a woman, for it is so clearly what I believe. Male, female—be who you are without the community's false notions on what it means to be either. I was pleased about this part of your letter because it revealed much about you. (Not that the rest of your letter didn't.) I understood from your first letters that you are a strong woman, emotionally and spiritually, sticking to academic subjects that were perceived as "boy" courses, taking leadership roles in various organizations. And that you are strongest when you are quiet, gentle, loving...no need to worry about being too anti-woman or not feminine enough. What does it mean to be a successful human being with the intellectual, social, spiritual, and physical advantages you have? Well, such success, in my way of thinking, is all about, as you wrote, being quiet (humble) and gentle (grace-filled) and loving (passionate).

Of course there is the mother side in you, the home side in you, the marriage side in you; but remember, Liz, you are blessed and cursed with that reflective nature. You have many talents; you have many choices. I see one of your challenges is to forge a life for yourself where your complete self is nurtured. My mother raised six children, one of whom was blind and completely mentally disabled. She came to this country not knowing any English, a vibrant woman filled with a will and a strength that was not perceived by her parents as grace. (My mother's father was a general in the Belgian army and was not very impressed that his daughter didn't want to attend prissy dinner parties and would rather stay home and read than visit Tante Margaret.) My mother came to America because of that will to be herself, to break out of the strict caste system that still exists in many ways in Belgium. My mother became a writer, balanced her everyday world with her passionate world in a way that helped her survive. My mother knows the upside-down kingdom and fought all her life to retain her place there, even in the seemingly never-ending burdens of motherhood and Oliver's disabilities.

William Carlos Williams was a family doctor in Rutherford, New Jersey. Wallace Stevens was an insurance executive in Hartford, Connecticut. Archibald MacLeish was a college professor, the Librarian of Congress, an advisor to Roosevelt. What do we do to tend to the muse in the everyday routines? That, it seems to me, is one of your biggest challenges and goals, to figure out just how you are going to balance being a woman with your talents, passions, and destiny.

You wrote that you always wanted to be tossed up in the sky as a child. Isn't that a wonderful metaphor that describes you perhaps? You want to be propelled up in the sky. Whose hands will help you rise? How will you handle the exhilaration of the journey up? What will you do when you see the beauty of the light upon the whole landscape from that perspective? Who will catch you when you come down?

I, like you, have little tolerance for small talk. I have one close male friend and a close woman friend, people to whom I can speak about *anything*. Such relationships, I find, are impossible to maintain with too many people, for it takes serious, important time to nurture such friendships. I have a solid, professional relationship with my teachers at work; cordial, even friendly and comfortable times with the neighbors. But what I like best is a deep friendship that is intimate, where I can be vulnerable and safe and feel that I am part of the other person.

I agree with you: I do believe we are born with much of who we are. God's instructions, perhaps? That you were smart as a child, that you weren't willing to earn poor grades for the attention of the boys, that you do not want limits placed upon you because you are a woman: all defines your power on the chessboard. The pawn can just move up and down, the knight in a diagonal line, the rook in a horizontal movement...but the queen, Liz, is the only piece in chess that can go in any direction she wants. What are little girls made of? What do young women think about? Depends on the little girl. Depends on the woman. Yes. Exactly. I think you are a queen.

Your age startles me because you have wisdom, the type of wisdom that comes with age and heartache and long winters and sleepless nights and tepid victories. I guess I always thought that a refined heart and intellect comes a few more years beyond twenty-one. To be sure, Willa Cather wrote that most of the material a writer uses is acquired before the age of fifteen, and there is much truth there. But Liz, look at yourself in the mirror and you will not find age. I am also pleased that it seems you do not know how refined and perceptive your letters are. I am just pleased that there are people your age who will surely take up the banner for the more difficult path in life, the harder way, the way of wind on the face.

And, yes, I think I misplace my delight...not in your age, as you suggest, but perhaps I am just a bit joyous that you are so much like me in many ways. But I was surely not me as much as I am today when I was twenty-one, and you are already so much you at twenty-one. I tell my honors and AP students at the beginning of the year, "You are all much smarter than I am." They giggle and think I am teasing them, but when I convince them that I am serious, I add, "I just have thirty years more reading and living experiences than you do. That is all." Perhaps too I do not surround myself with too many adults who have, as you say, bright eyes, dreams, and passion. The few intimate friends I have still retain this quality. So does my mother. It is difficult to find citizens of the upside-down kingdom. Perhaps that is one of the reasons why I am so delighted that you have come into my life. Something else: I think that you represent part of the ideal, part of the world that I have always believed existed. I have said this to other friends as well.

Concerning self and the reconciliation of a duality: For me there is no reconciliation, just a constant struggle to maintain a balance, whether that is the combination of the spirit and body, or desire and restrictions, or passion and the bills that have to be paid. I have recently been able to admit confidence in certain aspects of my life by looking back and seeing that for the past twenty-two years I have been a husband, father, teacher, and writer consistently, so that is probably what I am and probably what God intended me to be. Sometimes I want to be a columnist for *The Wall Street Journal* or a senator or a college professor; but in the main, I am with Roe and the children, drive to school each day, and write in the evening.

I sometimes fear that I am Willy Loman, just an ordinary pawn moving back and forth on the chessboard without much influence. T. S. Eliot has some wonderful lines in his poem "The Love Song of J. Alfred Prufrock" about this notion of being an unexceptional person, being common, not influential, and even at times like a fool. A man in a suit dreaming of sea-girls singing beyond the waves of the sea sounds like a ridiculous man, and at the same time he dreams about immortality.

The Greeks had it right in many ways with their belief in the gods and the gods' power to manipulate the weak creatures of the earth. We acknowledge, I think, that we experience waves of confidence at times when we feel a certain something in us that is unique, beautiful, lovely if you will. I think this a glimpse of what God created. If we believe we are created by God, well then, there must be some delightful components somewhere inside of us. That you feel restless about becoming who you truly are tells me you are already on the way.

You say that I sound content in my letters. Well, then I have managed to control my life and my doubts and my passions and regrets and deep joys. I wrote a poem about the two worlds: the world of the writer as he writes and the world of the writer as he does not write. What does the poet do when not writing a poem? I am constantly battling the storm within myself, conjuring up clouds and myths and women and goldfish. Anne Sexton's poems helped me write this piece. I need to be reminded that the ordinary, placed in the oil of the extraordinary, tends to create poetry. We choose each day to pursue milk or the sea monster each time we step out the door; and no matter what we choose, there is a lament.

I AM NO HERCULES

I could have begun a new storm within myself,
Conjured horses in clouds and the eyes of the hawk
In lightning shooting downward.
I could have prepared my own myths and gods
On rocking horse backs and goldfish seas
Where men invent victories and women
Sing in a tri-chorus.

But I was not brave under turning trees on my way to the
Milk store. All was gray and wet; the streets were
Silver sheets of water. I was heroic without boots.

I once had an invitation to ride the sea,
A frigate to China, unloading corn and wheat.
I even drove to the dock to see the size of the ship
And funnel; such a bow and the harbor smelled of
Oil and salt.
I could not leave my place
And pretend I was for adventure, so I became a
Teacher instead: no danger, no giant squid or
Typhoon, simply the routine of young men and young women
Leaning back in their chairs preparing for the sea themselves
Surely to make it upon the sea, that place where

They will go and feel the heave of waves and
Foreign smoke swirl around them.

I brought the sail of self down around my neck
To protect myself against the wind.
By the time I arrived at the store the rain had stopped.
My hair was flat. My coat smelled of wool.
"Caught in the storm?" the sales clerk said
As he rang up the jug of milk.

I was about to say tentacles of a sea monster,
Or the wild surf, instead I answered yes, and carried
The milk home in a brown paper bag.

Thank you for sharing that quotation from A. W. Tozer. What I like is your speaking about surrendering yourself to God and letting God be God. We leave ourselves vulnerable when we have complete trust in God; but in such helplessness there is a found strength, for that strength must be the love of God, a something that keeps us going.

I am trying to respond to each word you write, trying to write this letter in direct response to what you say in each line as if we were having a conversation. But when I come to the part where you address each significant notion of that quotation, I am at a loss as to how to respond, for there is so much moisture and soil and richness and murmuring from inside of you that it is impossible to keep up. I tell you, I am not very bright. I am more like a child than I am an adult, and I react to things in more of a childlike way than I do as an adult. I will just respond in a jumble. Risk your life on believing actively, yes. God is always looking out for you, yes. Liz, I also think you will never find true rest, nor will I. Knowledge can lead to pride, yes. Let us not waste truth, yes. Pursue the deepest life there is, yes. I see clearly why you use the word *compelled*, that you are driven, that you are insistent and passionate, yes. We must turn, choose the better way, give up our own will. (See, how does a twenty-one-year-old know this?) From the quotation and from your attention to each part that is significant to you, it is easy to tell that you say yes to life. You are a child of light.

Thank you for sharing that memory about the television campaign to raise money for the homeless that moved you when you were a little girl. I smiled when you talked about your history with God being murky after your childhood days. Good way to put it. I think, probably, that all of our histories with God are murky in one way or another.

The struggles your mother endured and the puzzlement about God's being in charge among all that is ugly do challenge a logical thinker. Anger in a congregation, divorce in a marriage, the persecution of the innocent, how could this be if God is in charge? Free will, Liz, and, yes, you are right, a merciful God. I believe that and have always believed that in the center of who I am. I believe that God is merciful. I think perhaps that God is like a parent. A parent loves his or her children unconditionally, offers guidance, ideals, sustenance, and sends the children into the world and hopes for the best. If the child succeeds, the parent opens her arms. If the child fails, the parent opens her arms. Having just said this, I continued to read your letter and found you saying the same thing about your own father. I see God as being someone like Atticus in *To Kill a Mockingbird*. That is my earthly vision of God. (Did you read that book? If not, I want to be the one to send you a copy.) I refuse to accept the notion that God is vengeful, frightening, Oz-like, and thunder. Jesus loved children. Your vision of what God is like is similar to mine. (Atticus, Liz, Atticus!) And yes, Liz, the quest. Yeats said that we slouch our way back to Bethlehem. Most great books I have read are about that quest, that journey to God. Although the metaphor is different in each book, the end is the same.

I am glad that these letters have already played a part in helping you articulate significant elements of who you are. Someday you will be able to read these letters objectively and see more clearly what I believe I already see in you, in

your writing, and in your female, young, Christian, Minnesota way of looking at the upside-down kingdom that
you have already stepped into.

I do think you are right in part about my attraction to
your first letter. You do sound like me, or the part of me
that I want to be like. I too have a hard time combining
spiritual convictions with the way things are. When I am
tired, all the sadness wells up in me. I am sometimes
tortured with the loneliness I feel, with the world's restrictions. When I am tired, I recognize that my writing will
never be as beautiful as Loren Eiseley's or Harper Lee's or
William Carlos Williams'. All my regrets well up in me
when I am exhausted: memories of lost friendships, of
Betty, of my grandmother who died thirteen years ago; all
surrounds me with a cloak of darkness. That you tell me so
quickly that you also endure such bouts with a lost sense of
self, well, that is comforting. We all seem to have cycles that
move us upward in the sky and that also pull us down.
"Up! Up!" a girl from Minnesota remembers saying when
she was little. I will tell you this: Every morning after a late
evening of sadness, every morning I feel rejuvenated and
hopeful all over again. I want to know about your sadness,
about the times when you are tired and worn out but especially about the times when you feel alone.

I like how you suggest that I ask questions or voice a dis-
agreement with something you have said. You like to grow,
prod, challenge, risk.

The Christmas holiday is finished. All over the village
people have discarded their Christmas trees onto the street
for ultimate collection. A mere three or four weeks ago we
stomped through a field of pine trees in Pennsylvania in
search of the prized tree, and now, so quickly it will be
turned out. We still have the tree in the family room, still
covered with lights and glass bulbs and angels made of
wood. Perhaps someone ought to create a six-foot porcelain
Christmas tree so that it can stay in the corner of the room
all year as an object of art, surely an object of delight. A

Christmas tree is much more appealing than an imitation seventeenth-century wingback chair.

Sitting on my desk here where I write are the Benedictine Monks of Santo Domingo de Silos on their CD, a book by Lewis Hyde called *The Gift* (all about the imagination and literature), my address book that is falling apart, my Dundee marmalade jar filled with my blue pens, a small Christmas gift—a Santa Claus carved from the tagua nut from the South American rain forest, my watch, two letters from Archibald MacLeish and one from Loren Eiseley. I have been cleaning out drawers and found these letters. I will never forget what I felt when these letters arrived in my mailbox: a sense of relief...they understand, they believe I am on the right track. My regret is never having met either MacLeish or Eiseley in person. Both men influenced my writing style. Both men reminded me of my own sad soul and the joy and pain it takes to tend to that soul.

Lewis Hyde wrote "Walt Whitman says that 'the inmost secrets of art' sleep between sympathy and pride....By 'pride' Whitman means not haughtiness but something closer to self-confidence." We can be sympathetic to the world and so embrace the world as wide as we can extend our own two arms. Self-confidence is created in the little advances we make toward self-preservation. We step out into the world and realize it has the ability to destroy us; yet if we do the right dance, acquire the right vocabulary, or maneuver in the right spot, we survive, and the world spins with us.

I quickly shaved this morning, leaving much of my face rough and dark. I do not intend to walk into the day's challenges with a mask of darkness on my face. An unshaved man is a man on the brink of a decision: to grow a beard or to look savage. I never grew a beard before, but there have been plenty of times when I wanted to look savage or feel savage or act savage. I have never learned how to play in a wild way, never taken any risks, never set out on an adventure that wasn't planned and safe. Sometimes when I am in a meeting, and I rub my hand against my cheek and feel a spot where I missed in my morning routine of shaving, I think about the trees outside the building or the distant mountains or the desert I will probably never see or the Nile or the Mississippi (I'd like to swim in the Mississippi someday) or my father's backyard as it was filled with wild onions and my sister dared me to eat one raw, which I never did. I do not know much about the inner secrets of art, but I know a great deal about the inner secrets of my own self, the secret desire, for example, to be rough and Hemingway-like. Ask a forty-seven-year-old man why he is walking the dog at 11:15 at night, and he will say, "Because the dog has to pee." I think the answer is that the man has to confront the darkness and the neighbor's savage oak trees leaning over the quiet street protected with a single lightbulb hanging from a telephone pole. Who has dared to spit in the dark or talk to the moon or cry while walking the dog at 11:15?

It is 9:40 in the evening. I've never figured out P.M. and A.M. where I can use this with confidence, so I say 9:40 in the evening. I don't think I even want to know for sure and with confidence the difference. It is the same with the body. I don't really want to know about livers and lungs and blood vessels. I'd rather imagine all that just happens some-how. I celebrate the possibilities of the body and what it does to maintain itself, but I don't want to be distracted with all the details. (I also faint easily.) I don't really want to know the inside of a day, A.M. or P.M. I am just pleased to see the sun's light in the morning and catch the moon sneaking through the trees at night.

I received a call from a woman who just finished reading some of my books. She said that she felt, all her life, that she had a piece missing inside of her. She said that she was abused as a child and never felt as if she had a childhood, and then she read some of my essays about my childhood memories. "I slept last night with a deep sense of peace after reading some of your book," she told me. She said she felt throughout her life that she was a wheel rolling along with a piece missing, and the wheel of herself bumped and bumped each time it turned on the ground of life. "I tried all my life to fill that missing piece with goodness. I felt lonely all my life, yet I have a husband and children. They are married and successful. I realized, after reading your book, that my loneliness was a gift, that if I didn't feel this missing piece of myself, I would not have gone off on a search trying to find out what was lost. I guess I became a better thinking person because I questioned so much in my life."

I suggested that we all retain this loneliness, or this inner feeling of loss or sadness. If she had the best childhood, the best marriage, the best children, the best health, there would still be that gnawing feeling inside of her. And, I said, there is also a sense of guilt. We have so much in our lives, and yet we are not happy. Or we feel a thorn of loss in our side. How dare we feel such a thing in the reality of all the suffering that goes on in the world around us right in our own neighborhood. So we live between the comfort of our circumstance and the agony of our feelings. But when we are less tired or not in the cycle of a physical discomfort, things seem good. We are carried by the joy of our feelings, and we accept our circumstance and peace in the recognition that the next bout of discomfort or the next difficult challenge will inevitably come. So we rock back and forth between the self we love and the self we do not love. When we eat crackers on the couch, the crumbs always collect between the cushions and later haunt us. Do we stop eating the crackers?

I said to the woman on the phone that she did not discover Chris de Vinck in my books. I said, "Dorothy, you found, as you read, five percent Chris de Vinck and 95 percent Dorothy. And that is one of a writer's victories." A book that is 95 percent the author makes for good house insulation after it is ground up in the shredder, which is where most books end up.

Well, I have gone on probably too much here, but when a writer finds a well, he or she likes to draw up the water.

Before I stop, I want to mention a few things. On April 8, Kelly Monroe, a chaplain from Harvard University will be speaking at North Park. We were speaking on the phone yesterday about what we have been doing, places we have gone, people we met. I spoke to her about meeting you and receiving your first letter last September, and then she said, "Oh, I'm giving a talk at North Park in April." She asked for your name, and she hopes to meet you. She is one of the writers who will be in my book on Henri Nouwen. She is bright, filled with her vocation as a minister; and she might be able to give you some guidance about your future. Are you applying to graduate school?

Something else. I was invited to give a talk in Chicago on February 21. I am arriving on February 17, that Wednesday night. Because I will be on vacation for the entire week, because Roe doesn't have the time off, and because the children are also in school, I thought I would combine my talk with visits to a number of friends in the Chicago area, and surely I was hoping to meet you.

I look forward to your next letter that will be, I hope, free of any restriction on my part. I would like to see your poem about the top fifteen people in your life. I am pleased that you like sappy movies. Did you see *Stepmom*? Roe and I were exhausted after seeing that film.

Do you know the work and writing of Dorothy Day?

I hope you someday read *The Brothers Karamazov* and by all means tell me about those dark, sad nights.

Thank you, Liz, for your friendship and for your careful attention to my letters, and to me. I "shan't" deny that I like the idea that both you and the Mississippi began in Minnesota.

Christopher

Letter Eleven

"To fall in love is love is easy..."

"To fall in love is very easy, even to remain in it is not difficult; our human loneliness is cause enough. But it is a hard quest worth making to find a comrade through whose presence one becomes steadily the person one desires to be."

—Anna Louise Strong
I Change Worlds

Dear Christopher:

What a month! What a beautiful, full, transitional month I have been having! My thoughts are ripe to be recorded and shipped off to you before they spoil and burst. But where to begin?

I apologize that it has been so long since you've received written correspondence from me. I admit that talking to you on your visit in Chicago makes writing seem so inefficient; you can get so much more done talking than you can writing! But, then again, there is a *quality* in writing that the *quantity* of speaking doesn't surpass. It was wonderful to meet you.

Thank you again for a fun afternoon, for letting me hear the phone message from Fred Rogers, for not minding my fast Chicago driving, and for letting me see how your face looks when you are thinking and talking about something.

I told Peter about the "art exhibit" at the museum that I stormed into the library to see, and the grin you had as you told me the title of the display! I thought a lot about what we talked about, especially what you said about Peter, about you and Roe, and the feelings/thoughts that we think we need and the ones that we actually do need to be in a relationship with someone. That is something that many people talked to me about these last few weeks. But I will talk to you more about that later. First, let me respond to some of the questions and things that you wrote in the last letter.

I have been hit on all sides lately with how much my reflective nature, as you call it, defines me! Right now I am typing to you from a friend's house in California, where my dear friend Kara and I have been lounging around for three days. Our spring break from college was last week, and she and I left almost two feet of soggy, brown snow with all our luggage, proceeded to get stranded in Cincinnati for *five hours*, and arrived in California around midnight to be picked up by different friends at the airport. I left the next morning on the train for Denver to visit a close friend of mine from my high school youth group (one of the women who tops my list of friends who have dramatically changed who I am). We had a wonderful time talking, laughing, and shopping together. We hiked up a little mountain trail, took lots of pictures, and walked through card and candle stores.

I also had a wonderful time on the train itself; for two days and one night I rambled between my coach seat, the observation car (floor to ceiling windows and swivel couches), the diner car, and the lounges below where people could smoke or chat or watch movies. It got tiresome, and sleeping crunched on the seat wasn't the best arrangement, but I met some incredible people and saw beautiful countryside. We zoomed right through a pass in a range that cuts through the northeastern part of California. I spent hours looking over ridges, into valleys, up steep purple scaffolds, and seeing heavy snow drifts covering trees, bushes, and shrubs.

I *love* the mountains, as I think I told you, and it felt surreal to watch these towering rocks and beautiful flowers under the changing sun and its shadows. I played a CD of my brother's high school honors choir part of the time I was looking out the window; hearing a cappella chants and longing, baroque harmonies was relaxing and fit the panorama that steadily moved before me.

That was part of the fun of taking the train: just sitting and absorbing and thinking. The other part was the people that I met, like Sheryl, who is a pastor's wife in Utah and has had over thirty foster children. She ministers to all kinds of people in the church who have been abused, addicted to drugs or alcohol, or who have alternate styles of dress and who are not generally accepted by many churches. I almost cried several times in our three-hour conversation as I

130

listened to the compassion and simple devotion she has for her congregation and family. And I met Farrok, who is of the Baha'i faith, who explained to me his ideas about how to have a strong family and bring God's kingdom here on earth and how science and technology play into it. I had never heard of this faith before and learned a lot about how other people see success and goals and how God saves people. Farrok believes that it is primarily through following the laws and by working hard and bringing the greater peace to people every day, the greater peace—showing love and mercy to others as God would.

And there were other people whom I shared ten minutes or an hour with who were interesting, caring people. It was nice to be forced to slow down, to read or talk or look out the window or listen to music but not to be able to run around or make a bunch of phone calls or create a to-do list. (I confess I had a running check-off list the whole vacation, but the items were different like, "send Peter a postcard" or "call Mom from the next station" or "get a copy of a map.") Yep, some things never change. I wanted to be efficient and strategic and not waste time even on my trip.

After Denver I went to Seattle and saw the better part of Whidbey Island with a friend in the Navy. We toured wharves and art exhibits; followed trails through overgrown parks and along beaches; enjoyed coastlines bordered by mountains and rocky ledges; went through tourist shops, open-air markets of fish, flowers, and souvenirs; and dined on British tea, Mediterranean seafood, and the occasional McDonald's meal! Seattle was beautiful, and contrary to what I had heard before my trip, it did not rain for the two full days I was there and only drizzled the morning I left. Seattle was a hurried, eclectic, caffeine-supported place (every six stores or so downtown was a coffee store; I am not exaggerating).

Then I took the train through Washington, Oregon, and northern California, and ended up here near Sacramento. Just yesterday morning I was watching the sun rise over the purple, misty Sierra mountains in the distance and seeing the orange and red glare through rows and rows of dainty, pink-blossomed fruit trees. We must have traveled through fifty miles of cherry, walnut, almond, apple, and plum trees along the train route, and this time of year they are all in bloom. My mother calls such flowering trees "Mother's Day Trees" because in Minnesota they almost always show their beautiful colors the weekend of Mother's Day.

Now I am here in California with Kara, with many friends and miles and meals and mountains behind me, resting up and relaxing before we head out to visit a few more friends in Utah and attend a national conference for colleges involved in service. We will meet seven students from our college there and go to workshops, plan for next year, get some vision and renewed passion, and just have some plain old fun, I am sure!

It has been such a wonderful time traveling by train, plane, ferry, car, Jeep® , bus, and on foot around the north-western part of our country. Just watching the changing landscape as we coasted from succulent and flowering farmland in California to the dried-out Nevada dust towns to the rocky, arid, green frontier of Colorado—that was all worth the cheap tickets! Visiting with people I have known or just met was, of course, the reason for it all; and simply seeing life from another perspective was invaluable.

People are so darn interesting! They have so much beauty in how they talk or in what they care about or in what they take time to explain to you. Maybe all of America should take a big road trip together, bonding and relaxing and seeing all the gorgeous land and population. I had never been farther west than Colorado before, and I loved this experience and hope to return sometime. You can probably tell that I love to travel, and it sounds like you get to do that often; so this may sound common in a way, but I feel so lucky to be able to travel like this. I adore the journey, both inwardly and outwardly, and I wanted to share it with you. And of course I couldn't type on the train.

Let me answer some of your previous questions. The books I received for Christmas that I am reading (before the one you gave me!) are *The Jesus I Never Knew* by Philip Yancey (which is marvelous, by the way), *Reaching Out* by Henri Nouwen (have you heard of this author somewhere, perhaps?), and *The Power of One* by Bryce Courtenay.

The first two books are my typical reading choices: nonfiction and inspirational. The third is the book that a movie was based on that describes life in South Africa under apartheid in the 1940s and 1950s. I also received some cute Christian inspirational books, one called *Hugs* and one about the life and writing of Rich Mullins (an author, songwriter, and performer who died recently). He wrote lyrics of depth, and he moved to a Native American reservation to live out his convictions, teaching and serving the children of that community. I am encouraged by his faith and passionate words. He died in a car crash and his last CD was finished by friends in the Christian recording community, a beautiful addition to my collection.

And no, I have not read *To Kill a Mockingbird* yet!

Kara is calling my name from downstairs. We're going to some bookstores and eating Mexican before seeing the movie *October Sky*, so I have to go. I am not sure when I will finish this.

Well, it is much later, two weeks, and I am compiling the parts of the letter that I already wrote you, so I apologize if it seems disjointed. The rest of my trip was memorable. I saw some close friends from high school, toured the Temple of the Church of Latter Day Saints in Salt Lake City, and ate yummy daiquiri-rum-flavored Baskin-Robbins ice cream. The conference was productive and beneficial, especially for those who will be running the Urban Outreach programs here at North Park next year. I told the other students that I was suffering from "UO withdrawal." Of all the places and things on campus, that office, those people, and that mission is what I will miss the most. I realized that when I was there I felt organized, in charge, and passionate. At UO I was affirmed and given leadership, and I was a teacher. I felt like I was doing something of eternal significance that was needed and acknowledged. It was at times challenging and frustrating, but it was what I was good at. This is what I need to look for these next few years when I am planning my career; I assume that is what everyone needs.

I hope that I can help others find that job, that niche where they are themselves and excited and pushed to do new things and to think in new ways. I think that I want to work on a college campus eventually. There is great potential in influencing the minds that will lead the future. Just think how powerful it is to influence even ten other people to serve and volunteer and commit their time to others each year, if they are then trained in how to spread that passion for service to others.

Anyway, I loved the conference and since then have been brainstorming about my future and what choices and options I have. But there is another big part of my last month that will affect my future that I have not told you about yet. This part of the letter could just be called the "Peter Letter," simply because I am going to go on and on about him and about our relationship! This is what has taken up the other half of my time. (Yes, another excuse for why you have not received mail from me in a while.)

The two weeks following your visit were ones full of thinking and debating, talking late at night and praying even later into the night! There were so many things that kept tugging at my heart about my relationship with Peter: I no longer wanted to go away for a year or more and "be on my own," doing mission work or fulfilling my ambitious independent streak. I didn't want to date other people in search of the "perfect mate," fulfilling my childhood visions of exactly what a husband should look like and be. I didn't want to have the choice to go wherever and do whatever I wanted without the "burden" of a husband and his decisions. I didn't even fear the idea of commitment and the final "for-the-rest-of-your-life" decision that marriage would bring anymore.

But these things all changed slowly, most of them starting at the beginning of this year, many of them culminating in my thoughts, feelings, and discussions over Christmas break and shortly afterwards. It was odd, but I could tell that I was being drawn toward Peter, drawn toward being committed to him.

I had Matt talk to me about listening to my heart and my emotions. He said that I should not stay in the "middle phase" for too long because that meant I was teetering between deciding what I really wanted and just assuming that things would always be as they are.

My friend Tim reminded me that love is something that draws you into it: part of it is logical but part of it you don't decide; it just attracts you, and you want to be a part of it.

Kara reminded me of the true definition of a Christian: someone who serves and loves others without thought of himself or herself. Being a Christian isn't easy or fun or relaxing or even necessarily healthy much of the time. It means giving things up, appearing weak to others, and doing what you think would bring glory to God, even if that doesn't line up with what would pump up the latest mega-church or leadership program or money campaign. (Those things aren't necessarily bad, but they should not be the focus of a disciple's life.) This is the kind of Christian that Peter is.

I spoke with Tom about the "resume" qualities of a boyfriend/girlfriend and how we would like to be able to parade each other around saying, "she/he is the richest or smartest or cutest or most athletic, and she/he is all mine!" We concluded that it is your relationship with someone that is crucial, not the list of attractive personal traits; but we also realized that internally, we would have to be ready to "give up" the secret hope of finding that resume in someone that we love.

I talked to my brother Timmy about Peter, and I heard him say that he knows that Peter cares about me and other people and will always be the kind of man I need in my life. He also said that Peter is fun and smart and good with others and that when we are both grown up and married, our families should plan vacations together for fun. (That has always been one of our goals! I was glad that he saw Peter fitting into that.)

I spoke with my one close married friend, Kristin, about the battles of living with someone, living with the disappointment that you usually work through in the first year of marriage, and the ways a solid church or small group of friends help support that initial growth. She said that if Peter and I took a class with other couples or a compatibility test, we would realize that we're far advanced in a relationship that is based on lifelong qualities.

Peter and I talked about how there is a "list" that you look for in a spouse but that once you really love someone and you desire to change/be changed by them, the list almost has to disappear. Otherwise you love someone for being profound or organized or gentle or aggressive. What if he or she stops being that way? What if one of you is depressed or injured or life just doesn't go the way you think it will? What is the point of being married if you are not committing to that person, no matter who he or she becomes? (We made allowances if someone turned abusive or changed so much that it truly harms the spouse, but what many claim in divorce courts as "harm" can be as little as a reduced standard of living. That is ridiculous.)

I kept feeling drawn to being with Peter. I wasn't frightened or feeling pressure. I didn't see him as a hindrance to my freedom. I didn't worry that someone else was better. I wanted him. So the weekend of February 21, I asked Peter if he thought it was at all possible to get married this summer. He gave me an incredulous look and said something about how it was probably possible, but why was I thinking about that anyway? He has been in the position of waiting and not wanting to pressure me for a while now. In order not to push me more than I was ready for, he hadn't even thought ahead about when we would realistically get married, how it would work out with future plans, etc. In our conversation we tackled all the big issues that we could think of: finances, where and when the wedding would be, what we would do this summer, what we would do for the next five years down the road, opportunities for graduate school and mission trips, what our families would probably say—whatever questions came to mind regarding committing to someone for the rest of our lives!

In one way it was surreal and unnatural, talking about issues like "when we have kids" or "when we have a house." In another sense it was exciting and almost normal, as if this was the next step that we had logically progressed to and the way that we are with each other was almost set up for these conversations. (Even after disagreements, Peter would laugh and say, "I even love fighting with you. We always get a lot accomplished because we communicate clearly and I learn new things about you!")

We decided to spend a week praying, thinking about, and really being thorough about any problems, fears, questions, or insecurities we had about our considering engagement. We each confided in one close friend on campus to give us a more well-rounded perspective. It was a week when I was forever changed, and I don't know how to say it less dramatically than that.

I dredged up every concern, every diluted ideal, every spiritual question that I had in my mental files and worked through them all. It was what somcone like myself has to do in order to commit to something as big as marriage. Stupid questions like "Am I ready to share a room and space with someone?" Huge life issues like "Would I regret this decision if I met someone later on in life who was more of something I had always wanted?" The whole gambit was thought through. I tried to answer all of these questions by listening to my mind and my heart, a tricky combination for me as I am more prone to rely on logic and realistic lists than my swaying emotions.

Saturday night, February 27, Peter took me to an African restaurant. It was the perfect mix of a formal setting (linen napkins, goblets, wine-colored tablecloths) and a fun atmosphere (masks on the walls, upbeat music, personable staff). Peter prayed right after our exotic food arrived at the table, and his words had already made me teary-eyed: "Thank you so much for the blessing of my relationship with Liz, for the way that she has taught me about you, for all the love and growth that we have experienced together." He looked up at me from the prayer and almost whispered, "I really want to ask you to marry me right now!" He had the most precious, tender look … and he asked … and I said yes. Then we went to the symphony together and heard Dvorak and Mozart. All through the concert I was staring at the beautiful solitaire ring as it reflected sparkles against the light. Peter kept rubbing his hand over my fourth finger, feeling the new shape adorning my hand.

I called my parents from a restaurant after the concert and yelled over the noise of the bar that we were engaged. They were excited and yelled back, "Congratulations." We rode the El home and smiled and laughed and held each other along the frost-covered sidewalk. And that is the story of how I finally got engaged!

I have been thinking about all the details: planning a wedding, organizing the ceremony and reception, and who to invite and how to make it beautiful and meaningful … all those fun things. But even more important than that, I have been thinking about being married, being a wife, starting a new phase in my life. One friend wrote me a card with congratulations and a note reminding me not to forget her. My brother is writing a song that he'll perform at the wedding, and so far it is about losing his sister because she is all grown up. I am receiving pamphlets in the mail from cake companies, photography agencies, flower businesses, and invitation catalogs. Peter's sister bought me a bridal magazine and stated that Peter and I were soul mates. When talking about my future, I use the pronoun "we." It is real. I am actually getting married.

It is an incredible, exciting time but as is often true, the joy is close to sadness too. I will miss my brother and the way that we always knocked on the wall in code to say "good night" or "come to my room" or "I love you." I will miss having a room of my own and decorating it in "girlie" colors and blaring my music late into the night. I will miss not having many of my responsibilities covered by others and having to really worry about bills and insurance and food and rent on my own. I still feel like I am eighteen most of the time. I know that parts of me are dying; they have grown old and aren't as active any more, and they are being replaced by "The Adult Liz"! And then I feel like I am growing up, which makes me feel tired and like I should know more than I do.

One woman at our church said that she always thought that before she became a mother she would know more, be more ready than she was. But motherhood happened. She had a child and in the process became a mother. I think that is how things in life are. No one really gives us manuals on how things should go, but we become more and more of who we already are, and then that is what makes us a mother or wife or whatever it is that we are becoming.

A song I like says "It's not what I am finding out; it's what I know." But things are not going as I had always planned that they would. I never thought I would be married until I was at least twenty-four or twenty-five. I thought I would be on my own, live single, and be self-sufficient. I thought that I would receive a divine postcard with specific instructions about who to marry, when, and how it all should work out. But I will be married one month after turning twenty-two. I will get married right after college, as do all those people that I used to make fun of. I have received no postcard from heaven clearly spelling out my future. But I want to be with Peter. And I think that this desire was influenced by heaven.

Every question, every concern about my life, or about what kind of person I should be or what kind of a family I will have—I would rather answer it with him than with anyone else, or even by myself. He is the person who knows every facet of my personality, my weaknesses and prejudices, my particular assumptions and goals concerning the future, and he still loves all of it! I like wandering through stores, entertaining friends, being crabby after a disappointment, staying up late talking about everything, and doing nothing in particular, better when it is with him. I realized that no matter where we go or what problems we face, we have the skills to work through our lives together. We communicate well with each other. We listen and care about male/female roles. We spend money and time in roughly the same ways, and our ability to connect on big issues like our faith, church, volunteering, and politics are all comparable.

All of these things are somewhat logical and, I think, important aspects of what kind of love you need to have to be married. But they are all revolving around what really convinced me to marry Peter, this best friend and great person I have had in my life for several years and now have decided to change into my one and only life partner. I realized what love meant to me.

You said something when you visited about the kind of feeling that I had, maybe always expected to have, when I was in love. Yes, I thought that I would be devastated if he wasn't around for five minutes or that every time I looked at him I would recall all the traits that would always make me certain that I had found the perfect man. Not only did I realize that that was not ever going to happen (and wasn't even a healthy goal ... I think you should be able to be without your spouse for five minutes), I had a change of mind-set as to the definition of love.

For me, love means wanting to give up part of who I am in order to be joined with someone else. That is a hard phrase to interpret correctly because I am not giving up in the negative, resigning sense; but I am choosing not to fully exercise all of the parts of myself that I could if I were single. For instance, I realized that even if I never get to go to Hungary and do mission work, even if I never have a job that I find significant and challenging, even if I never get to travel or go through more schooling, that's OK if I get to be with Peter. That doesn't mean that I don't still have those goals or that he doesn't have his own, but I think that part of love is agreeing that the other person is more important than you are. Their wants and dreams are yours now, and that realistically limits options in some ways; and it also introduces a whole new collection of options in other ways.

Professor John Bray, a good friend of both of ours who is officiating the ceremony, always says that marriage is the biggest change agent in one's life. I think that is true. For me, realizing I was ready to be changed, to alter my goals and my plans and "the way I always thought life would go" played a big part in getting engaged. This is closely tied to the other big reason that I realized I really loved Peter: He makes me more of me. Even though I know that I will change a lot, even though I am ready and even excited about the possibility of growing and learning with Peter, I know that his effect on me is to help me be more of who I want to be—more than I could ever become on my own! He makes me more of who I *hope* to be, who I think I *could* be. He reminds me of that deep inside part of me, and he nurtures it—even when I can't do this for myself.

This is a quote Kara found this week from a book by Anna Louise Strong. I am considering using it on the front of our wedding invitations: "To fall in love is very easy, even to remain in it is not difficult; our human loneliness is cause enough. But it is a hard quest worth making to find a comrade through whose presence one becomes steadily the person one desires to be."

I have always secretly felt that falling in love, that magical fate that every young girl and boy hopes for, is really more a perception and a wish than it is a reality. Not that the fantasy isn't powerful or wonderful or true in some sense, but why can people "love" someone who abuses them? Why don't people "love" the obvious friends and supporters in their lives who sacrifice for them? How can married couples operate as if they are in a business, ferrying kids to school and sports, balancing checkbooks, and landscaping the yards, but have no real relationship with each other? How do some people fall in love for thirty, forty, fifty years in committed, healthy marriages, and other people who seem to have it all together separate after three years? Did you wonder about these things before marrying Roe? I don't mean to sound cynical. I know that you can be busy and drive your kids places and still have a great marriage. I guess I just keenly remember witnessing several exceptions to the ideal of love and marriage, and after that I could not assume that two friendly, balanced, attractive, Christian people would automatically have a joy-filled, predictably great marriage.

I am a twenty-one-year-old, and as my mother reminds me, I don't always know as much as I think I do. So my theories on lifetime commitment could be really off base. But I am fighting, the only way that I know how, the notion that you are guaranteed a happy, comfortable life if you do certain things. Even if you love someone and really try to show him that and create an idyllic life, there is no guarantee that you will have an ideal life. Even if you are a Christian and marry another Christian and commit all that you do to the Lord, that does not mean that you will never have heartache or poverty or death or pain. Even if you are intelligent and plan ahead and, if you remember my first letter, are "educated, organized, and socially adjusted" that does not mean you will necessarily get to experience intimacy or spirituality with your spouse or in life to its fullest. So why do we tell people in books and movies and even in some churches that there are guarantees? My life has not even been very hard, and I can still tell you that reality does not work that way.

By marrying Peter I am choosing certain things in life. I am choosing to be with someone who is not the highest on the world's scale of success but who listens to me and loves and supports my life. I am choosing not to aim at attaining the highest financial security possible, but I have no doubt that he cares about me and about my dreams even more than I do. I am not choosing someone who will manipulate people and push to get ahead and to get his way, but I will be with someone who models sacrificial love and who serves others and pushes me to be like that as well. I am choosing someone whom I know and have invested in, not some attractive stranger with whom I don't know what life will be like. I always thought I would want more of a daring, adventurous relationship, but this comfortable friend of over three years has turned into being exactly what I want. Once someone told me that I would have to decide if I wanted a specific kind of man (an unrealistic abstract list) or Peter. I've made my choice. I want Peter. The wedding will be September 5, the Sunday of Labor Day weekend, in the evening.

See what I meant when I said that this would be a good letter? I had a lot going on and I still do: planning this summer and the wedding and where to live, what work we will find. Oh yes, and I am still in school and that means that I should be doing homework too somewhere in that schedule. Pray that I continue to cherish *today* in the midst of all this planning for *tomorrow*. I have so much more that I am thinking about, but I will write on those thoughts later. I want to get this letter actually sent to you. I have missed our monthly discussions and want to hear your thoughts concerning our marriage. Tell me what you think about influencing the future by influencing people. As a teacher that is what you are doing every day. How do you show your students how to be the best that is inside of them?

Take care, my friend, and keep being a tame sea-monster under that pleasant, shaved, teacher-Sequa face. (I liked the poem.) I think every human being who is honest with himself or herself struggles with that very issue. Until next time, God bless.

Letter Twelve

The power of Love

When I said yes to Roe in my own heart, all the pain was immediately lifted. We struggle with our vocations; we struggle with God's will. If we are open to what God is leading us to, we can easily be sick, for we tend to make war in our hearts between what we want and what God wants. The trick is to know who is doing the talking.

Dear Liz:

Most of the best things in my life come to me without warning.
I looked so often for a letter from you; and then when my disappointment grew and grew, I began to check the mailbox less
and less with specific hope. (I always anticipate the mail.) I
returned from my first ride this season in my Model A Ford.
After I turned off the engine, cut off the gas, and stepped out of
the car, I thought about checking the mail. The forsythia are in
bloom: silent, still, yellow flames along the driveway. When I
pulled out the day's mail I shuffled through it. Bill. Junk. Bill.
Advertisement. Letter. YOU! Such a wonderful surprise. I sat on
the stoop and opened the envelope immediately.

The front stoop is one of my favorite places to read. I
don't read novels there or any other book that is an ongoing
project. I like to read the newspaper and letters on the front
stoop, morsels to be eaten slowly. I read books mostly beside
the lamp in the small living room, the chair closest to the
door. But I did read *At Home in the World* by Joyce Maynard as
I sat on the western side of the couch during the Christmas
vacation. The landscape of my life, while small, does not
diminish my pleasure at the expanse I feel when I am in the
middle of a good book or a good letter. A letter from Chicago
transports me to Chicago.

I was pleased to read the first words of your letter: "What
a month!" And that it is—a month of transition. I was anticipating your explaining what has happened, and you did not
disappoint. Do not apologize, never apologize for any
delayed response to anything I send you. Letters to friends

ought to be sent out of love and never duty. I can always tell when someone writes to me because they feel that they are obligated according to some unwritten rule of etiquette. Those letters are like reading Tennyson...same old thing. But a letter written from desire or passion or love or friendship or delight or loneliness or will, well, those letters sound like Virginia Woolf. (I was disturbed this past weekend for it was when I learned that Virginia Woolf committed suicide. I was so sad to hear this, as if it happened yesterday. Well, for me, she did die in such a horrible way yesterday.)

Thank you for spending so much time with me during my stay in Chicago. The speech was a success, our time at the museum memorable; your voice, laughter, physical presence a perfect match to what I had imagined. I was impressed with how comfortable you seemed to be with yourself and with me. It is a wonderful thing to meet someone for the first time in person and to feel immediately at ease; to feel, well, who you are on the inside. That we were able to grow a little in our friendship through our letters before we met did add to the wonderful comfort I felt when we first said hello.

You will see with me, perhaps, that the writing self doesn't match the speaking self...or perhaps you will find just the opposite. I feel like a much richer person of the heart when I write, where I can respond in silence to so much that is not silent in my life. I like the variety of choices we have to extend ourselves personally to others: letters, speaking, a twist of the head, silence in the presence of those we care for.

I am glad that your reflective nature has been fired up this month. Shows you are ember-alive. You will always feel this burning. I was pleased to hear that you wrote much of this newest letter in California. (My, you do get around! Denver, Cincinnati, Chicago, California, Washington, Oregon, Minnesota. My front stoop sounds more and more relaxing.) Tell me someday about that friend in Colorado who dramatically changed who you are.

As I read your letter I felt as if I was walking with you in the little shop of cards and candles. Those stores are all the same across the country: a clean smell, balloons and cards, chocolate arranged here and there in order, and glass shelves. I also liked sitting with you in the train to Denver.

There is something sad about being in a train. Going somewhere, feeling the movement, leaning my head against the glass window as landscapes, houses, cities flicker past me. Last summer we took a train from Brussels to Brugge. We were on the same tracks my mother and father were on when they went on their honeymoon fifty-three years ago.

The war was still bleeding Europe. Bombs were falling around the train, but my parents arrived safely in Brugge in the middle of the night. The station was empty. The city was in the black. Air raid regulations forced everyone to extinguish their lights. As my mother and father walked from the station to the city, they saw in the distance a single yellow light. They followed this light, which brought them to the police station. My father spoke to the sergeant at the desk, asking directions to their hotel. The policeman gave perfectly good directions and, as my father thanked him and began to turn, the officer asked, "But where are you going?" My father explained that he was taking his bride to the hotel. The policeman looked at the newlyweds and said, "But I am sorry. You cannot wander about the city. There is a curfew." He looked at my father, then said, "If you'd like, you can spend the night in the cell. There is a bed there." My father was indignant, saying that he would not spend the first night of his marriage in a jail cell. "Suit yourself," the policeman said, and he then pointed to a bench down the hall.

My mother and father dragged their two bags to the bench and sat down. They were exhausted and discouraged, but then my father had an idea. He stood up, quietly walked down the hall and out the building. In a moment he came back to my mother, picked up the two bags, and led my mother quietly out of the police station. There was a huge, black car parked behind the building. My father opened the back door and he and my mother crawled in, spread out as best they could on the back seat, and fell asleep immediately.

They were awakened the next morning by the roaring voice of a huge, angry man. "What are you doing in my car? Get out! Get out!" It turned out that the car belonged to the chief of police, a man lacking in any humor or sympathy. Eventually my parents made their way to their hotel. (My oldest brother was born exactly nine months later.)

You discovered much that makes America what it is: the physical features of a continent crowded with mountains and open territory, cities and parks. When I read this portion of your letter, I thought of Yugoslavia and the bombings. Most of us in this country do not know what it is like to have planes fly overhead and drop explosives. We do not know what it is like to be forced from our homes with nothing. My parents knew this so well, of course, during World War II.

So good to see Philip Yancey among your Christmas gifts. He is in my book about Henri Nouwen. I met Philip, finally, in person last year at a conference. He gave the morning talk, and I gave the afternoon talk. I told him how much I admire his writing. I like very much the way he is able to collect information, do research, read a variety of things, then bring that all together with his own insights as he moves a theme throughout a book. He has brought the message of the good news to many people. He lives outside of Denver, I believe. And you also received one of Henri's books for Christmas … and you are going to meet Kelly Monroe… all these people who come together in my book.

Ah! You don't have *To Kill a Mockingbird*! Wonderful. I will send you a copy. I received in the mail a few weeks ago the thirty-fifth anniversary edition of the novel signed by Harper Lee. I bought it at an auction, and I am pleased to have it. I don't collect many autographs. The books I have that are autographed are from writers I have met or befriended. To a very few I send their books and ask for an autograph. I like to have a bit of the writer. Of course what they write is more than their signature, but there is something appealing about having someone's signature. It is physical proof that they were attentive for a few seconds to this or that particular piece of paper. I particularly wanted an autographed copy of Lee's book, for she was one of the most influential writers in my life.

Daiquiri-rum-flavored Baskin Robbins ice cream? I am a basic chocolate man myself. I annoy my younger brother each time we go out for ice cream together. He believes in taking risks, trying exotic flavors. When I am asked for my order, and I say "chocolate," my brother rolls his eyes. In many ways I am a boring person.

Yes, you will be leaving Urban Outreach. I suppose this is the beginning of your journey, your recognition that everything comes to an end somehow. Fitzgerald tells us this in *The Great Gatsby*. It is a wonder that we human beings start anything, realizing that nothing lasts. The first time I experienced this was when I graduated from high school. I finally began to feel that I had found my place, understood who I was, begun to make friends, then suddenly, high school was over. It hurt me so much that I never kept in touch with anyone from that time in my life, and I never attended any of the class reunions. I've worked in six school districts in my life, met wonderful people, established meaningful, professional relationships, yet I've never returned to any of the schools where I have been. Partly I don't have the time to keep up with all the people I met along the way, but I also know that what is gone is gone forever. All that is left are memories. What has lasted in my life: my family, my writing. Neither has hurt me. In memory of your work with Urban Outreach, I am also enclosing Robert Coles's book for you: *The Call of Service*.

Congratulations! Congratulations! Congratulations on your engagement! I wanted to say this to you at the beginning of the letter, but I also wanted to respond to you in the order I received your words. I believe a letter exchange, a true letter exchange, is a dialogue. When I write to you I feel as if I am talking to you, responding to your thoughts. It seems to me that you are beginning to form a clear view of what love looks like. It is difficult, I believe, for someone your age to come to this realization fully; for in order to see the entire marriage, the staying power, the meaning, you will have to see it to its end, which will hopefully be in seventy or eighty years.

Perhaps I can speak of marriage in the form of a parable. In 1940 my grandfather was a colonel in the Belgian army. At the beginning of World War II he barely escaped Brussels as the Nazi troops stormed into the city. He was forced to leave my mother and my grandmother behind. They were relatively safe in the city. There was no coal to heat the house and only small portions of black bread and weak soup to keep them alive, but these conditions were better than trying to escape through the battlefields.

Within a few days, two officers came to my grandmother's house, banged on the door, and barked, "Where is the colonel?" My grandmother gave a quick, clever response as they searched the house. "That bum! He ran off with a woman. I hope you catch him before I do!"

The black-uniformed soldiers snickered, looked around once more, stepped out of the house, and never returned.

For two years my grandmother did not know what had happened to my grandfather; so many people were displaced and killed during the invasion. There were no letters. There was no telephone communication. Radios were forbidden, but my mother, a teenager at the time, listened just the same.

Late one night, as my mother pressed her ear to the speaker and turned the radio to its lowest volume, she heard a faint voice from the BBC encouraging people to hold on, not to give up hope. "Mom! Mom!" my mother shouted, "Come listen!" My grandmother leaned over the small radio as the vacuum tubes glowed in the dark.

"We are not defeated. Resist as best you can!" It was the voice of my grandfather, and it was the first time that my grandmother knew that he was still alive. He had been captured in Spain and imprisoned. He then had escaped and made his way to England where he spent the war years working for the resistance movement in London.

Every second summer when I was a child, my grand-mother and grandfather sailed to America to spend six months with us in New Jersey. They walked arm in arm to church each Sunday. They sat together on the lawn chairs in the sun and read the newspaper. They liked to go food shop-ping and test the melons together.

In 1973 my grandfather died in his sleep. For ten more years my grandmother flew to America on a jumbo jet to join us for the summer months.

One evening, during the last months she was with us, I helped my grandmother up to her room, as was the routine; then we sat on her bed and talked. She unclipped her large mother-of-pearl earrings. I helped her unfasten her white bead necklace, then she slipped off her watch, a heavy man's watch. As she began to carefully wind the watch, she whis-pered, "Your grandfather died nine years ago. This is his watch, and it has been running nonstop since his death." We both looked closely at the small second hand tick-tick-tick-ing. "I wind it each night and it makes me feel as if I still have a part of your grandfather with me."

It was impossible to separate my grandparents no matter how hard the world tried. This is the staying power, the hope of such a relationship, which you are just beginning to dis-cover with Peter, and this is good.

No one can know for sure if a marriage will survive, and I think the world these days increases the odds against a lasting marriage. But I remember Alan Alda saying in a television interview about the endurance of his marriage, "Hey, a deal is a deal." A vow is a vow. A promise is a promise. We make a promise in our traditional marriage ceremony to move forward together. "We two form a multitude," the famous book *The Family of Man* uses so well throughout the text. In your letter you say, "And this is the story of how I finally got engaged!" The wonder of it all is that the story is just beginning. You will tell your children someday about February 27, 1999.

I thought your list of things that make you similar hints at the foundation of your relationship. Roe and I knew that we both felt comfortable at being who we are in the presence of each other. We both knew we loved each other without conditions. We too have similar attitudes about children and God. Is there a "perfect" one to marry? No. Are there many, many people you could fall in love with and marry? Of course. Why do some marriages last a lifetime, while others end in three years? I cannot answer all this. I feel in many ways that people who marry for all the right reasons do so because of grace.

Are you and Peter going to struggle in your marriage? Yes, of course. Will there be things that happen that could threaten your relationship with him someday? By all means. Will there be pain, suffering, anger? No doubt. Ah, but also there will be days, years, moments that will bind your relationship. Each year you will build something between the two of you that no one else can destroy. There will be joy and passion and deep holiness. Life, Liz, life will work upon you and Peter, with all its mercurial wiles, with all its tricks and surprises; but my grandmother kept that watch ticking and ticking.

What should a starting couple know about? Well, it seems as if you are well on your way to discovering this. It seems from what you have told me that much of the foundation of your relationship is already built on solid ground. Perhaps one of the best things is a willingness to grow and be open to growth in all the various parts of a marriage: intellectually, spiritually, sexually, and emotionally. All these things have a significant impact on a lasting marriage. That you are both college graduates and both readers speaks of a future where you will both continue to pursue experiences that will continue to enrich your minds. I often see high school couples where the boy might be very smart and the girl isn't interested in ideas … or I see couples where the opposite is true. Either way, a couple that is mismatched intellectually seems to be heading for trouble.

I think also that a starting couple ought to have a common spiritual bond. It is obvious that you and Peter have this already. If one person in the marriage doesn't have faith or doesn't pray or doesn't live a life of gratitude or a life of generosity, then the relationship is lopsided. If we do not have a developed spiritual side and we are not willing to move closer to God, and the other person is, then there can be tension and disappointment. It is odd to hear about a family where the husband or wife stays at home, and the rest of the family goes to church. When a man and woman join in marriage, they begin to build a community. When they have children, they add to that little community. How nice to live with people you love surrounded in the faith that heaven and God exist.

If a couple believes all comes from God, what a grand adventure they will have. Faith gives people a way of seeing that is much like the vision of a child. Michael, who is fourteen, still says aloud how much he likes seeing the cat sitting in the sun on the front stoop. You and Peter will see, together, a sunset or your child being born or the flowers growing in your garden, and because you have the vision of faith, you will feel a deep gratitude for such things; and this gratitude will be directed to God in celebration.

If you or Peter had no faith, it would be difficult to share in the gratitude together. If people do not know whom to thank, they can easily become selfish and arrogant. Do the things of this earth come to us from our own labors, or do they come through our own labors under the guidance and love of God?

Also, Liz, I think that grace plays an important role here. From what I have learned about you, I have no doubt that you have grace. And from what you have told me about Peter, it sounds as if he has grace too. I am not sure everyone has this, but I can recognize it when I see it. The spiritual quality of your relationship probably binds all else. Blaisé Pascal wrote, "The heart has its reasons which reason knows not. This is felt in a thousand ways. It is the heart that perceives God, not the mind. Such is perfect faith: God perceived by the heart." If only one person in a relationship has such a heart, the other is left out and lost.

My father said in his book, *The Yes Book*, that faith in God is a gift. It is offered to those who seek God in all good will and objectivity, knocking at the door of truth, hoping for an answer. My father reminded me that knocking may take a lifetime, or the door may open at first approach. There is no human reason why faith is so hard for some people and so easy for others. How lucky you are to have met a man who knocked and found faith as you have done. Some people struggle all their lives, fighting against God, or fighting with their doubts about God; and other people open the door and say, "Oh, there you are."

I think, also, that a starting couple ought to have great sensuality. In one of my favorite books *Diary 1928–1957*, Julian Green wrote, "Right in the twentieth century, our ideas of religion are so peculiar that one is not religious, in the eyes of the world, without also being ever so little of a puritan. For the devout, enemy number one is the sexual instinct; the only thing he forgets is that this instinct comes from God."

The final thing a new couple needs, I think, is emotional compatibility. If both people are low-keyed and dull, that is sad. If one person is full of life and optimism, and the other is depressed all the time, it would seem to me that the relationship will not survive.

One of my favorite books is *The Importance of Living* by Lin Yutang. I would quickly add this to your marriage library. Such a nice thought: when you marry, you can merge your books with Peter's and begin your own library. Yutang's book would make a terrific addition. Here is some advice he gives:

> Man, we are told, has aspirations. They are very laudable things to have, for aspirations are generally classified as noble. And why not? Whether as individuals or as nations, we all dream and act more or less in accordance with our dreams. Some dream a little more than others, as there is a child in every family who dreams more and perhaps one who dreams less. And I must confess to a secret partiality for the one who dreams. Generally he is the sadder one, but no

matter; he is also capable of greater joy and thrills and heights of ecstasy. For I think we are constituted like a receiving set for ideas, as radio sets are equipped for receiving music from the air. Some sets with a finer response pick up the finer short waves which are lost to the other sets, and why, of course, that finer, more distant music is all the more precious if only because it is less easily perceivable. And those dreams of our childhood, they are not so unreal as we might think. Somehow they stay with us through-out our life. That is why, if I had my choice of being any one author in the world, I would be Hans Christian Andersen rather than anybody else. To write the story of the Mermaid, or to be the Mermaid our-selves, thinking the Mermaid's thoughts and aspiring to be old enough to come up to the surface of the water, is to have felt one of the keenest and most beautiful delights that humanity is capable of....

I am excited for you, for you have made a choice. We make choices in our lives, and whom we marry is one of the most significant decisions. When I first met Roe, I was in great doubt inside myself, and that doubt led to misery and fear. For six months I struggled with our relationship. When I said yes to Roe in my own heart, all the pain was *immediately* lifted. We struggle with our vocations, we struggle with God's will. If we are open to what God is leading us to, we can eas-ily be sick, for we tend to make war in our hearts between what we want and what God wants. The trick is to know who is doing the talking.

So I send to you heaps of congratulations upon your engagement and the book *To Kill a Mockingbird* as an engage-ment gift. I don't know the exact date I asked Roe to marry me, but I do know that it was in the month of May.

Roe and I have been planting azaleas, turning the soil around the trees in preparation for the summer flowers, which we will plant next week. Our funny dog stretches out on the freshly-turned earth because it is cool against her belly.

With the fighting in eastern Europe, with the horrible killing of the students in Colorado we see again evidence of great evil. I thought once that evil was an actual thing, something, or someone real. To me it is more real than that. It is the absence of love. Where there is no love, the empty space is filled with the opposite. Where there is no moisture, there is the desert. Where there is no heat, there is the cold. Where there is no light, there is darkness. Where there is no love, there is hate. We need to fill our lives and the lives of our children with love, for such sustenance fills in the empty spaces in our hearts.

If children are given experiences filled with hate again and again, the children become hate. But if children are given experiences of love again and again, the children become love. The problem is that we have a world that doesn't give children love and hate equally, nor is this a world that gives both any kind of continuity that is easy. It is difficult to give a child the continuity of love day after day. That is the work, the vocation of parents. Once you and Peter marry, you publicly announce that you will be giving each other the continuity of love that will fill in the void in both your hearts. Someday you may have children, and they will be part of the central focus of your lives.

Let me tell you how Roe and I met.

I grew up in a cedar shaded, three-story colonial house in Allendale, a small town in the northeastern section of New Jersey, where the Erie Lackawanna train carried New York City commuters back and forth. There was still a place for a working farm. There were six churches and a place where you could buy the newspaper and rock candy. This town had one traffic light and two schools.

There was enough to occupy a boy in Allendale: swimming in the summer, ice-skating in the winter. I chased fire trucks on my bike and bought Good Humor® ice cream from the white truck that drove around the edges of the ball field.

After college, I returned to Allendale and became a teacher in the high school. The sound of the railroad didn't speak to me any longer. I stopped swimming and skating and chasing fire trucks. Something was missing.

In 1974 I was twenty-two years old, a high school English teacher, and a lonely young man. I had dated a number of women, but each time there was something missing in the relationship: laughter perhaps, serious intentions, fun, a deep sense of self and joy in the presence of the other person. I am not sure what was missing, but there was definite anguish in my life.

Much of my sadness was postponed each summer when my parents, my sisters, my brother, and I drove five hundred miles to our little cabin on a slow river two hours west of Ottawa, Canada. It was there that I learned how to swim as a boy, where I learned how to spend the afternoon picking raspberries, how to lean back on the sand of the beach and watch falling stars. This Canadian vacation was the highlight of our year: better than Christmas, better than birthdays.

One afternoon during that summer of 1974, while my family was spread out on the beach, I stood up from my towel and announced, simply, that I was going for a walk. I was grateful that no one wanted to join me. I had a plan.

"Be back for supper at 6:00," my mother suggested as I turned and waved. Then I walked along the driveway, down the dirt road, across an open field, and over to a small path that led to the paved road. Ten minutes later I stood before a small, open gate that stood before a wide path leading up a steep hill.

When I reached the top of the hill, I stood at the entrance to the smallest church I had ever known. This church was a shrine to a number of Canadian martyrs who died defending their religious beliefs. This chapel had four pews, four little windows, and a wide front door. This was a good place to make a deal with God.

"Now listen," I said aloud as I sat on the back pew, "I would like a wife. I've been a good person, I think. I am lonely. Can't you help me out here?" I asked God. "I'll make a deal." Then I stood up and reached in my back pocket and pulled out my wallet. "Here. Here is my college I.D. card from Columbia University. I am going to leave it above the door frame, and when I come back next year, I would like to come back and retrieve it with my bride. What do you say?"

Well, there was silence as I turned, walked to the rear of the chapel, reached up and placed my I.D. card on the top sill above the door, and then I began my journey back to the beach.

The vacation was over. We drove home. The summer ended. School began. The year passed quickly: Halloween, Christmas, winter, May flowers, and suddenly, once again, my family and I drove to Canada. We were all on the beach reading, playing cards, sunbathing when I, once again, announced that I wanted to take a walk.

I made my way down the dirt road and again across the open field, down the path, and finally to the small open gate. By the time I reached the entrance to the little chapel I was tired.

"OK, what happened?" I asked God. "Here I am a year later, and no girl." I reached up over the door sill and found my college I.D. card. It was covered in dust. I wiped it clean, turned to face the front of the chapel and said, "OK. I'll give you another chance. I'll once again leave my card over the door. Don't you understand? I'm lonely. You can help. Please, when I come back next year to retrieve my card, let me do it with my wife." Again, I reached over the door, placed the card flat on the sill, then I returned to the beach to rejoin my family.

The vacation swam peacefully to its conclusion, and we drove home. School once again. Halloween. November. I was in my classroom first period, taking attendance. "Barbara. Jack. Susan. Jeannie...? Has anyone seen Jeannie?"

"She's absent, Mr. de Vinck," someone said.

Jeannie. Senior class officer. Star of the school production "The Music Man," honor student, and absent from my class one foggy morning in November 1975. The day continued in a regular routine. Stories were read. Papers collected. Discussions were carried out. I didn't know that this day would change my life forever.

By fifth period I heard that there had been an accident. By seventh period I heard that Jeannie was driving. By the end of the day, everyone in school knew that Jeannie had died on the way to the hospital.

Jeannie was driving to school that morning in a light blue Duster. Her brother was in the front seat. Her neighbor was in the back. The morning sun was hidden by dense fog. Jeannie drove through the winding roads. When she came to the crossroads, she could see the blinking light in the thick, gray mist. She stopped, looked both ways, then pulled out cautiously into the intersection. At that moment, a car drove out through the fog to her left, and smashed into Jeannie's door. Her brother sustained a severe broken leg. The neighbor in the back seat was unharmed. Jeannie, the Music Man's bride, died at the age of seventeen.

Jeannie's parents, people of great faith and goodness, did not want a wake. They just wanted to embrace their community; so they opened their home for three days, and the community came: high school students, teachers, parents, neighbors, church congregations.

I drove to the house to honor my student and to add my condolences to the family. When I stepped inside, I noticed right away, sitting on the piano, Jeannie's graduation picture, a memory of all that was, and a shattered dream of all that could have been.

I spoke to Jeannie's mother and father, walked into the kitchen and stood quietly in the room with a number of my students. They were somber. I did the best I could to soothe their pain, and then there was a slight commotion at the front door. Jeannie's sister from college had just arrived with three roommates. There were tears and hugs and words of hope, and then the college girls entered the kitchen and stood beside me. The girl to my right, Roe, had long dark hair and wide, dark eyes.

As the sad day progressed, I made my way around the house, meeting people, greeting my students, being useful. Then I noticed that Roe was in the dining room.

People in the neighborhood brought all sorts of food: ham, soup, bread, cold cuts, sodas. I saw that Roe had a plate in her hand as I walked into the room. I grabbed a plate. The table was between us. I smiled. She looked up at me and smiled, then I said in a question, "Roe?" I was going to ask her for her phone number. Just as I was going to speak up, an old, old aunt hobbled into the dining room. I looked at Roe and simply walked out of the room. I just didn't have the courage to ask a girl out on a date with someone watching me.

At the end of the night a friend and I drove Roe home. When I said good-bye, she gave me her phone number, and the next day I called up the girl with long dark hair and wide dark eyes.

Roe was studying to be an elementary school teacher. She liked to read. She was interested in my brothers and sisters. She liked to plant flowers, take long walks. Roe liked the television program "The Waltons," babies, restaurants, and, best of all, she seemed to like me.

Roe and I dated for six months. We went on picnics, took the Erie Lackawanna railroad to New York City. I bought her ice cream, took her ice-skating. I probably would have chased fire trucks with her if she would have let me.

Time passed. I was visiting Roe at the house she and her five roommates rented for their last years in college. We had been dating for six months. We had spent the weekend together: visiting friends, eating at our favorite restaurant, going to a movie. Finally, on Sunday evening, it was time for me to go home. We were in the guest room. I was packing my bags when Roe asked, "Chris? Is there something you want to ask me?"

Roe and I had discussed marriage. "I was waiting to ask you in that little church in Canada." She just smiled. "Marry me, Roe," I said. She said yes. I gave her the ring I had carried with me for six weeks. We rushed downstairs to tell the roommates, then Roe and I took a walk in the cool, spring air.

I do not remember what we spoke about, but I do remember Roe saying, "Let's hop the fence," which she promptly did. It was a fence that surrounded an elementary school. I climbed the fence and followed Roe to a set of swings. She took the one to the right and I the one to the left, and as we began to swing back and forth we both chanted together, "We're getting married! We're getting married!"

The following summer, my family, Roe, and I drove five hundred miles to our Canadian river. One hot afternoon on the beach, I whispered to Roe, "Let's go for a walk." She and I left the family drinking lemonade on the beach as I led her down the road, across the wide field, and up the hill to the chapel. We stepped inside and thanked God for our engagement, and just before we walked out, I reached up to retrieve my I.D. card, but this time it was gone. Things are taken away and given to us for the most unlikely reasons.

Who gave me the gift of my wife? God? Well yes, but also a seventeen-year-old girl who died at the crossroads in the fog long ago. Jeannie's family knows that from the deep sadness in their lives something good happened: Roe and I met. We celebrate our twenty-second wedding anniversary this year. We have three children.

Roe and I still swing back and forth together on any swing set we can find, and we return to the little chapel each summer where I say a prayer, in thanks, for Jeannie, the "Music Man's" lady librarian; for Jeannie, this man's lady of hope and salvation. Thank you, Jeannie, for Roe and for my children.

Stability in your marriage, Liz, will create stability of love for your children. They will grow in that love, and they will learn and pass it along to their children. Remember, it was discovered in this century that the Neanderthals liked flowers. That is a good sign. We have a long tradition of something gentle in our genes.

You and Peter are blessed.

Christopher

Letter Thirteen

faith is
a choice

I am thankful for my thinking and for my questions and for my rational convictions about faith and biblical research in school. I am thankful for my graduation from my Bible-camp faith to my more realistic beliefs. But believing is not about knowing, and faith is not about security. It is about loving God, and I feel this more this year than I did last year. I want to be alone with God and to listen more to what God is saying. Even as I struggle to make that a habit and to live out that relationship with God, I want to. *Faith is choice.*

Dear Christopher:

Can you believe it? You are receiving another letter from your long lost friend in Chicago! And I am here, once again, in the city, actually living two blocks away from where my apartment was last year, one block east of the Swedish restaurant where you and I dined when you visited the city! I have been thinking and praying and growing up so much lately, and I want to tell you about some of it. But first, I should give you the news update that you deserve after too many months of no correspondence. But, no, I feel myself wanting to be non-specific and jump into the deep vague things that are happening in my heart. I hope you can follow!

I am Mrs. VerHage now. I am fully married, betrothed, taken, committed, pledged, decided, and, yes, can carry the title of "wife." I know that people get married every day, all over the world, and almost as many people end their marriages or are forced to end them each day as well ... but there is a magical quality about marriage that I never believed was truly there.

I liked so much hearing about how you and Roe met. You know from our letters that I do not "believe" in love as many do, and I cannot swallow the silly ideas that marriage ends all problems, solves all issues of self-worth, and brings a divine, mystical "rightness" to our existence. I think that marriage is a decision and a vocation that involves work and rational thinking; but there is also something magical when I look into the hazel eyes of the same person first thing in the morning, every morning, and his are the last eyes I see before I fall asleep every night.

Loving Peter is one of the most fulfilling things that I have done. It is not being loved *by* him that brings me satisfaction; it is what I have learned about loving back, being fundamentally changed and enriched as a person by giving up a part of myself for another person. Did you ever see the film *Marvin's Room*? There is a part where Diane Keaton's character explains, through tender tears, that her rich life was so wonderful not because she *received* the love of her ailing aunt and sickly father, but because she could *give* them love, give them a part of herself. I know I must sound like a newlywed with all my words of magic and happiness, but I intend to write similar things when I am fifty. I love being married! Can you believe me, all emotional and sappy?

It was about a year ago that I wrote you the first letter. I was debating so many things: my career choices, my schooling, my faith. I was questioning my relationship with Peter, which was a comfort and a rich base to my life even then; but I had a long way to go before I could honestly say most of what I am saying now about love and marriage and giving and receiving. I think that is why I have missed you lately. I am feeling the same way that I always end up feeling in the fall. It is the season when the leaves swirl, when wool sweaters and mittens are pulled out from storage; it is the time of pumpkins and the smell of spice. It is a time of melancholy and reflection, winter on the way, everything closes and dies and sleeps; and yet autumn is fresh and crisp, which gives me a push to move and change and improve and start something, like a letter, like questions that are never answered.

This is the season when I return to thinking about the story of your brother Oliver, how he lived the thirty-two years of his life in bed, blind, mute, silent; and how you brought that story to my college campus and how it compelled me to write to you, compelled me to say thank you for corroborating much of what I feel about the small, significant wonders that I find hard to express. I remember I lit my favorite spice candle the first time that I wrote you a letter.

I remember being consumed by your book about Oliver because it spoke honestly and harshly about giving instead of receiving. (How did Diane Keaton know?) More than health or happiness or admiration or intelligence or even self-sufficiency, we need to give.

I can hardly organize my thinking to express it all to you. My summer was layered with significance. Graduation was an important step, but only one of many to come. My time in South Africa was emotionally and spiritually full and draining. I find it difficult to justify returning to my lifestyle in the United States that is so removed from the physical distress and poverty that exists in that sad part of the world. It doesn't feel right. How do I make a dent in the world's problems? How do I wrestle with the question that maybe the goal is not the answer but instead the process? In other words, the solution of sending the struggling poor money and food and textbooks might not be as important as the process I go through to witness that need of theirs. The feeling of their pain, their situations, the break from my own life might be more troublesome to deal with than the economic and practical issues. I pray that I will never stop trying to solve their everyday needs, as that clearly communicates the gospel and the love that all pain should evoke; but I cannot solve every problem and should not be disillusioned into thinking that I can. So what can I do? Listen and cry with them, and help those I meet in my daily life who need food for the soul. I feel like that may not be enough though.

I spent the summer in Minnesota with my parents and with my brother who is now a senior in high school. I loved our quick phone call this summer. You caught me in the middle of packing and sorting, as one is prone to do before moving and getting married. I looked through old scrapbooks and letters, spent the nights playing games and chatting with old friends, and made calls about apartments, wedding details, and job hunts back in Chicago.

Planning a wedding is not that difficult if you stick closely to the main points: love and vows. I had a few days when I was overwhelmed, but Peter's assurance and his calming voice carried me through. In the main, I found the whole process itself to be fun: talking with old friends, appreciating the personalities and abilities of my family, and anticipating the start of this new phase in my life. Everything went beautifully. The dress, bouquets, candles on the pews, tuxedos, the chorus singing a cappella from the back balcony, the sermon about becoming one, the vows where Peter cried and I spoke softly—it was all beautiful. Alicia, Peter's sister, wrote a poem about us—and how her pain of losing a brother was combined with the joy of gaining a sister. And my brother Tim wrote a song and performed it (guitar and singing). The chorus goes like this: "Remember the memories, when I look upon your face, you helped me when I fell down, here comes a new tomorrow, and I know it will be better than the last." (Everyone cried during those two moments.) And there was the symbolic Frisbee toss up the aisle with the rings tied on to it—our group of friends in college always played midnight Ultimate Frisbee, which resulted in bonding, good, dirty, sweaty fun, and lots of late-night talks. So the Frisbee (which was later signed and presented to Peter by the guys) represented a creative and fun humor break in the service, a meaningful and thoughtful tie-in from our marriage to our collective friendships.

We took a fun drive on the main street of our little town, Broadway, following the service and after popping hundreds of balloons that filled the back seat of my parents' car. (Our thoughtful friends taped tacks to the windows for this very purpose.) My brother whisked us to the reception, which was bathed in candlelight, surrounded by live piano music, filled with sweet desserts and so many supportive friends and family members.

We had people stand up and offer memorable and touching dedications. I had a surprise song sung to Peter called "The Things I Cannot Say." The song is about a girl who stores up all the impressive and touching moments about the man she loves in her heart but cannot tell the one she loves "because people like me find it hard to speak of things they cannot say." It was about her falling in love with all the beauty she saw in the man and then finally telling him so. Peter loved it.

We stayed late and helped clean up and danced impromptu to swing music and talked with all our college friends until the early morning hours. We saw family and friends the day after, opened gifts, and had a fun, relaxing week at a cabin in the Georgia foothills.

The thing that was the most special about the wedding was the way that everyone gave to it and enjoyed it and loved it like his or her own special day. A woman I had known since I was in elementary school handmade my dress; friends in the church took care of everything—housing college students, throwing me a shower, decorating the church for the reception, hosting a pool party, and serving the food. We had my piano teacher of ten years perform all the music, and a man who stood up for my dad in their wedding played the trumpet. Two close high school friends performed violin and voice solos. Our wedding was a weekend event, an ongoing fun time really to see people and to catch up and relax. Peter and I both felt that we experienced the truth of a community. We both felt affirmed as we were surrounded with care and love. I wish all people the same amount of happiness and contentment on their wedding day.

We also experienced another reception for all the Michigan family and church friends two weeks later. It was a beautiful and fun day. We rode on an antique fire engine, had a scrumptious homemade cake, and had a house full of supportive friends.

This fall was a time of transition, to say the least. We moved to Chicago and started working at four jobs between the two of us. Peter is at our university, teaching half-time in the Biology labs and working half-time for the computer service center doing administrative work. I am working full-time at Covenant Offices down the street from campus, which is the national, denominational headquarters for the church and college. It is not what I expected my after-college job would be. I have an office cubicle, and I work on a database and have to wear panty hose every day! But I am learning, slowly, that my gut feeling about taking this position in the first place was correct. I am meeting extraordinary people who have true, servant hearts and exciting passions and visions for the Covenant denomination. I am impressed with the church's ability to change and challenge and support the denomination's members. I am surprised at what God is teaching me, and I am making my job into a new job. I get to meet people who have the gifts to write and read and speak and learn and pray and plan ... and it all inspires me to exercise those same things. And I am learning to be humble. I quickly see that every job is important and every job that I do is a witness to what I *could* do, and it tells a little bit about me and about what I value.

The other job that Peter and I are enjoying together is with a group called "Jesus People USA." They are a community of Christians born out of the seventies revolution of faith and drastic lifestyle changes, and their main mission is to live for Christ full-time in every lifestyle choice that they make. They live in an apartment complex and share their incomes, meals, clothes, living space, worship, schooling, jobs, mission work—everything. They have changed the downtown area where they live by creating a shelter and a daytime soup kitchen. They care for the elderly, have open worship services, and have helped improve the businesses in the community. They do much good work with little pretense. And they do not pressure others to follow their lifestyle.

One specific mission that they support is called "Concerned Crafts," the business that we are beginning to work for. Its manager began this mission after feeling called to help support the poorest of the poor whom he encountered while traveling in Mexico. The first group he met were Guatemalan refugees. He brings the handcrafted work of this poor community and sells it here in the United States at a reasonable price, and then he sends the profits back to the people in Mexico. It is spiritually revealing to be involved in the care of the poor in this small way. I find that being around people who are not consumed with the typical American lifestyle is good for me. This work is also good for Peter and me as a couple, as we slowly combine our priorities and values and money and time and faith. How do we all, as a community, balance the struggle between money, comfort, and pleasure with those who have so little? How does anyone find the line between giving and going into debt? between trusting God to provide resources and becoming a mooch on those with steady incomes and investments? between being a person for others, as Jesus was called, and making space for responsibilities and alone time? I know that my own, inner contentment will not come from a college degree or from a title or even from an accomplishment, but it is hard to give up those worldly goals. They are not necessarily wrong, but they are not, it seems to me, the goals themselves.

So you see, I am in the same place, in all the important ways, that I was when I first wrote to you. I am thinking much about relationships and faith and about the reality of living out my life and being truly content and fulfilled in it, in this world.

Remember the notion of the upside-down kingdom? I still want to go by that scale, but it is easy to back out of it. What if it is hard or I have the wrong motivations or I am not listening enough? Will I remain sensitive enough to be able to discern the rules of that kingdom? I constantly see things as I think they *should* be, and sometimes the gap between that and the way things really *are* is heartbreaking, especially when I see the gap as it exists inside of my own soul and mind.

I still want to ask you about how you discern these things, how you really live out your ideals and the lessons that you learned from your mother and from Oliver, and how you teach that to your students and to your own children. I still want to feel that I am not alone in my pursuit and to hear others call out, "Yes, this is the right road. You will find what you are looking for. That longing in your heart is there and it will not be satisfied by any false kingdom." I still need to know that my pursuit is valid and worthy and honorable and holy...and yet I think I already know these answers. I think I am just afraid to say them aloud.

I guess if one truly important thing has changed this past year, it has been my acceptance of my true need to know God. I have the same questions, and I suspect that I will be asking them all of my life. Maybe every swirling leaf of every fall will call me to these questions and doubts and joys. Maybe that is the process: to struggle and fall and think and stand and pray and celebrate—to struggle again, all in faith under a merciful God. Maybe that is the process so that I *can't* focus on a goal, so that I *can't* neatly wrap up my life's purpose into a role or into a category. I am not particularly sure where I am going or how I am going to get there (though I struggle daily as I try to plan out every inch of that path!). But I feel more and more certain that I belong to God. My sense of rightness is slowly becoming more entwined with being with God. I have a long way to go, Chris, and I am glad that I get my whole life to travel that way...that way to God.

I am thankful for my thinking and for my questions and for my rational convictions about faith and biblical research in school. I am thankful for my graduation from my Bible-camp faith to my more realistic beliefs. But believing is not about knowing, and faith is not about security. It is about loving God, and I feel this more this year than I did last year. I want to be alone with God and to listen more to what God is saying. Even as I struggle to make that a habit and to live out that relationship with God, *I want to*. Faith is choice. I know that my answers are in God and in my realization that my life is really not my own. I realize this a little more each day. I realize that trying to own my life exclusively and selfishly for me does not get me anywhere.

I am growing tired, and my hands are feeling the strain of writing here to you this evening. I can tell that I have not written in some time. I want to tell you, that as I thought about our friendship and about our letter-writing habits and all that I have been able to mull over and work through between our correspondence, I am genuinely thankful for you and for your investment in this . . . in me. I miss the long, provoking epistles arriving from Pompton Plains.

I hope this letter was able to give you the updates on some of the important and practical details of my life in the present to convey the deeper thinking stages that I once again find myself in. I would love to ask you more about some things I am researching and trying to figure out regarding jobs and schooling and church issues that I am thinking through. But this is all that I can do tonight.

I would love to know how you are doing, as well. And your latest book on Henri Nouwen, is it out? Is it a wonderful success? I want to hear how your high school students are doing and how your son's second year at Rutgers has started off and what you're learning in your faith and your ideals and if you still talk with Mr. Rogers every week! And I appreciate the wedding present and kind card and the thoughtfulness. The silver and wood cross hangs in the living room now and blends with the African artwork and the cherry bookshelves very nicely.

I am sending you a few extra wedding pictures, some blurry or with funny expressions, since the reprints are not back yet and sometimes the formal photographs don't capture the mood anyway. See the group shot of the wedding party? I have a great look, huh? (Funny.) In the front row, third from the left, is Peter's Korean sister, Jill. Next to Peter is his brother Josh, and two girls to the right of me, with head slightly tilted, is his sister, Alicia. In the back row, with his brown head of hair directly over Alicia is my brother, Tim. This picture was taken by my aunt before the wedding. We got most of the candid pictures and group shots much cheaper since family members took them. The "Just Married" shot with the car shows some of the balloon remnants! And the group sitting down at the table kind of shows the mood at the reception. And the last picture, well, that one is of Peter and me.

I wish you well, and I hope you can understand my rambling. I have thought of you often and am glad to finally send you something to explain myself again. I would love to hear from you soon.

Oh, and my favorite quote that I heard this week was from someone I had lunch with. He said, "When you finally are in the place that God wants you to be, you will find that God has supplied you with all the skills that you need." What a great concept for me and for others in this phase of life as we struggle to hear a "calling" or struggle to find a direction. God will supply us, and that is what I keep learning.

Take care, my friend, and God bless you and your family.

Liz Mosbo VerHage ☺

Epilogue

This book, like a wrinkled photo from my summers at
Bible camp, is a snapshot from a certain point in my life. It
chronicles the musings and questions of my senior year in
college as I struggled to define who to become, what to do,
where to go—and most importantly, *why*...

This is not my final theology or answer to life. I am just
beginning this journey called "growing up." Do I truly want
to put others before myself? Do I want to love and serve and
give, instead of succeed, impress, and control? I began graduate work in seminary this fall, here in Chicago. I am pursuing my not-so-marketable passions of understanding more
about God's word and learning about the nonprofit service
world. I continue to learn how to be a wife and companion,
and I am daily amazed at how much Peter loves me. We are
balancing everyday life with the ideals—paying the bills,
solving conflicts, volunteering, getting the groceries, sharing
from our hearts. My brother comes over to play cards and
laugh and stay up late talking. We make dinners for our
friends and take weekend trips together and ask, "How are
you *really* doing?" I still hear from Chris occasionally, and
we talk about life, love, friends, vocation. I write articles
every once in a while about issues or a news assignment. I
guess it's true that some things do not change.

If contemplating my journey can assist you, then this
endeavor was made worthy. I pray that you may receive this
book as a gift, as a bridge to our common search for God
and the wide arms that give *rest* and *benediction* in
this chaotic life. For that is how our God works, in the
ordinariness of everyday people, in small words strung

compelled to write to you

together between New Jersey and Chicago, by the coincidences and graces of each "insignificant" day.

Liz Mosbo VerHage
October 2000
Chicago, Illinois

discussion/reflection guide

LETTER 1. *The Upside-Down Kingdom*

1. When have you envisioned an ideal such as the "upside-down kingdom"? In what ways do you think that those who are "powerless" can have power? Is power a positive or negative force?

2. Do you struggle with thinking that you are extraordinary? Would you consider yourself "above average" or "below average" or "average"? Where would you like to be?

3. Consider people you know who, though not obviously in power, you would consider extraordinary. Why? How have you conveyed your admirable opinion of them?

LETTER 2. *The Inside Self*

1. How do you open up your "inside self" to others? In what experiences has that self been accepted? rejected? strengthened?

2. How do you understand the ideal of sacrifice? Do you desire *more* of this attribute in your life or do you see it as wasteful or harmful?

3. When have you felt "compelled" to do things—speak to someone, go somewhere, write something? When have you acted on that feeling? What things do you feel compelled toward now that you believe you should follow up on?

LETTER 3. *Traveling Down a Different Path*

1. What decisions are you presently facing in this period of your life? Do you think that choosing a certain path will change you profoundly? Will it affect your inner self? your outer appearance?

2. What process do you experience when making decisions? Is God a part of that process? If so, how does God factor in?

3. What impending decisions might affect your inner self? Who could help you consider this aspect?

LETTER 4. *Where Do I Go from Here?*

1. What activities, geographic locations, or specific people bring out the "real you"? Why do those things/places/people evoke that response from you?

2. Trace the impact that your childhood has had on your life. What people or events left the deepest impressions on who you are today? How have you thanked those who left a positive mark?

3. Which unresolved feelings from negative childhood experiences impact you today? Who can help you sort through those feelings and address those issues?

LETTER 5. *Contentment and Passion*

1. What percentage of the time would you label yourself as content? as passionate? How would you like these percentages to differ? Why?

2. Would you characterize most of your choices as *safe, smart,* or just *feel right*? Explain how you came to make choices this way.

3. If you are in or have been in a romantic relationship, how has the *reality* of that relationship compared to your expectations or ideals of it? When do you know that you are with the right person, either for the short term or the long term?

4. What does the Bible have to say about struggling with contentment? about making decisions? How would this apply in your life?

LETTER 6. *Confidence and a Pure Heart*

1. Do you easily trust new friendships? Do you have many not-so-close friends or a few very close ones? Do either of these issues relate to your confidence in yourself?

2. Do you pursue God or does God pursue you? Why do you see it that way?

3. Have you witnessed "God-made" and "human-made" laws in a church or other setting? How are each beneficial? detrimental?

LETTER 9. *The Quest*

1. Do you think that "God spreads providential circumstances" in your life? Give examples. What part of the Tozer quote would you highlight or notice the most?

2. When have you experienced disappointment with Christians or with the institutional church? What do you do with those feelings? How do you feel about voicing them?

3. Do you think you can discern from the outside what a person's belief is on the inside? What does a person's marriage, friendships, job, etc., tell you about his or her faith? What can it *not* tell you?

4. Do you understand your faith to be an event, a daily process, or a presence that comes and goes? Do you believe there is any "right" way to experience faith?

LETTER 10. *The Delights of Friendship*

1. How many people do you feel truly comfortable being with? Do you think that others feel comfortable being around you? What factors go into this?

2. Where do you see evidence of a "design" in life? Do you think that there are reasons/designs behind suffering or disappointments?

3. With what "dualities of the self" do you struggle? Do you feel as if most people grasp all of who you are or just certain facets?

LETTER 11. *"To Fall in Love Is Easy..."*

1. What do you do to relax, vacation, or take a respite from everyday life? What effects do you see in yourself when you do *not* take time for that rest?

2. Can you think of couples that you would say are "made for each other"? Or couples who do not seem to "fit" together at all? What qualities would put a couple in that first group in your mind? in the second?

3. How does your perception of what love should be affect the reality of love that you have experienced? How has your personal experience caused you to redefine your ideas about love?

4. What are the pitfalls in believing that "true love" is out there? Are there problems with believing that true love does *not* exist? In your experience, how is it possible to remain both hopeful and realistic in the search for true love?

LETTER 12. *The Power of Love*

1. What changes (for better or for worse), do you see in today's societal ideas about marriage compared to how the institution was viewed twenty, forty, or sixty years ago?

2. How do you know that you are right when you have made a decision? Do you tend to waffle on your choice or do you move on without worrying about it? Do you think that there are indeed *right* and *wrong* choices in life? How do you define what is right and what is wrong?

LETTER 13. *Faith Is a Choice*

1. Do you honestly feel as if you need God to survive? What contributes to your feelings of need for God? What contributes to your feelings of independence or competence on your own?

2. Consider a time when you noticeably grew toward or away from God. What contributed to your response to God? What did you learn from your experience?

3. In what ways is faith a conscious choice for you? In what respects is faith "given" from another source and not under your control? How do these two aspects of faith interact in your life?